NAES COLLEGE LIBRARY
2838 WEST PETERSON
CHICAGO, IL 60659

DATE DUE

```
Book HS 01 Weston
Weston, Drake
Guidebook for Alcoholics
```

GUIDEBOOK FOR ALCOHOLICS

GUIDEBOOK FOR ALCOHOLICS

How to Succeed Without Drinking

by

Drake Weston, Ph.D.

EXPOSITION PRESS   NEW YORK

EXPOSITION PRESS INC., 386 Park Avenue South, New York 10016

FIRST EDITION

© 1964 by Drake Weston. *All rights reserved, including the right of reproduction in whole or in part in any form, except for short quotations in critical essays and reviews.* Manufactured in the United States of America.

EP 42133

Contents

Introduction	7
What Is an Alcoholic?	11
A Bit of Autobiography	13
Alcoholics Anonymous (A.A.)	15
A.A. Open Meetings	17
A.A. Closed Meetings	19
Are Special Types of A.A. Meetings Needed?	22
Why Not Try a Topic Meeting?	23
How to Have a Ferocious A.A. Meeting	25
How About a Soothing A.A. Meeting?	27
Holding an S.M.A. (Seldom Mention Alcohol) Meeting	28
Alcoholism as a Disease	29
More Autobiography (The D.T.s This Time)	32
Perfection Does Not Exist	34
How Many Meetings?	35
Thirteen Steps to Alcoholism	37
Signs of a Developing Alcoholic Disturbance	39
Total Abstinence the Only Remedy	41
How to Start Arresting Alcoholism	42
The Twenty-four Hour Plan	44
The A.A. Twelve Steps and How They Came About	46
Commentary on the Twelve Suggested Steps	51
Don't Get Hungry, Don't Get Thirsty, Don't Get Tired	55
Three Possible Points	56

The A.A. Slogans	58
Slips	60
Keep It as Simple as You Can	63
The R-A-G Emotions: Resentment, Anxiety, and Guilt	66
Resentment	68
Guilt	70
Anxiety	74
Windup on the R-A-G Emotions	76
Three Mental Mechanisms: R-I-P	79
Retroflection	80
Introjection	82
Projection	86
Three Stages to Despair: I-F-D	88
Psychotherapy and Alcoholism	90
Where Do We Go From Here?	95
First Steps in Self-Psychotherapy	97
What Will the Neighbors Say?	99
Hitting Bottom	102
"The Tyranny of the Should"	105
Life Is Not Fair!	110
More on Those Terrible Resentments	113
Stay in the Driver's Seat—But Drive Safely!	116
The Myerson Maneuver	118
No Magic Formula Exists	121
The Theory of Partial Solutions	123
The McGoldrick and Tracy Approaches	125
The National Council on Alcoholism	127
The Pill Problem	128
Some Ghastly Doggerel to Finish the Book	132
The End at Last	136

Introduction

This book is written for persons with alcoholic disturbances, by an arrested alcoholic who has been through the mill of disastrous drinking in times past. I have not taken a drink for several years. If I could drink without getting into trouble, I would; but since I can't, I have built up a habit of doing without alcohol. Bits of personal history are related here and there, but mainly this book deals with the various possible methods of arresting alcoholism.

There are two main approaches to the widespread problem of alcoholism. Single drinkers can be dealt with on an individual basis, as is the practice of many psychiatrists and psychologists. Or else groups of people can be gathered together and subjected to various doctrines intended to help their alcoholic situation. Since the best-known group approach is Alcoholics Anonymous (A.A.), I shall have much to say about their set of methods.

The psychological and similar approaches in this book are only possibilities. I lay no claim to being an expert in the field. But in dealing with my own alcoholism, I found it absolutely necessary to obtain the aid of psychiatry and to investigate many other recourses, as well as attending numerous Alcoholics Anonymous meetings.

I think that I am right when I say that the final arrest of my alcoholic deterioration can be attributed about one-third to psychiatry and psychology, one-third to A.A., and one-third to a lot of other things that I dug out of philosophy, logic, religion, sociology, and other fields.

This book may upset a number of people, especially those who think that they already have all the answers. That can't be helped. Indeed, it may be salutary to shake things up a bit. A Chinese sage once wrote a book that received adverse criticism. His comment was, "If I had waited until my book was perfect, I would have waited forever." If I tried to write a book that would please everybody, I would end by pleasing nobody, least of all myself.

A condition like alcoholism runs out to infinity, and the last word can never be spoken. Whoever dislikes any of the possible methods that I outline is at liberty to do exactly the opposite of what I suggest. Or else he can do something entirely different. Almost anything that people find helpful in dealing with their alcoholic and other disturbances can be recommended. But in any case it is imperative to *do something*, to take some action, however painful it may be.

DRAKE WESTON

GUIDEBOOK FOR ALCOHOLICS

What Is an Alcoholic?

What is an alcoholic? An interesting question, and perhaps I ought to be able to come up with a slick answer. Unfortunately, I can't. I drank alcohol excessively for years. Finally, I was able to stop, partly through several kinds of psychiatry, partly through Alcoholics Anonymous, and partly by cultivating other interests that shifted my thoughts and emotional reactions away from alcohol.

The currently prevailing idea in A.A. is that there are two kinds of drinkers: the "social drinker," who never gets into too much trouble (though he may get drunk now and then), and the "alcoholic drinker," who cannot take one or two drinks, but once he gets started must have more and more until he ends in some disaster, great or small. According to a current A.A. theory, there is some sort of invisible line of demarcation between the two categories. Once the social drinker has passed over this alleged invisible line, he is no longer a social drinker but a full-fledged alcoholic, whether he admits it or not.

This is a simple way of looking at things; but perhaps it is too simple and out of line with the facts. I have heard endless discussions at A.A. meetings on what an alcoholic is or is not, and just how and when and where the mysterious invisible line is crossed.

In my opinion, and it is only that, the invisible line does not exist at all in most cases. Merely saying that something exists is not proof that it exists. You must demonstrate it in some fashion. In a minority of cases an emotional shock seems to touch off excessive drinking; but then the line is certainly not invisible, but obvious. Probably most of us drifted into excessive drinking rather slowly and over a period of years.

I am inclined to think that it is a waste of time and brain power to try to decide whether a person merits the label or designation of "alcoholic." The alcoholic state may be fairly evident or it may not be. I have seen too many mixed-up, doubtful, borderline cases to want to make a diagnosis of them. Just where one state shades into the other no one can say with any certainty. It is like trying to decide at just what point a baby becomes a child, or a middle-aged man becomes old.

What often happens is that in early life a person can drink alcohol without too much trouble; but as the years go by, consumption is stepped up and up until disturbances follow. For some, the progression is slow; a steady drinker may die of old age before getting into serious trouble. For others, the progression is very fast. I have even heard of people who began drinking late in life but progressed so rapidly that in a matter of months, or even weeks, they had an alcoholic problem.

We can make a kind of parable about it. If you are out in the middle of the Atlantic Ocean in a boat and you sail due north, it is impossible to say just where you cross the Arctic Circle unless you engage in astronomical observations, and even then you may not be quite certain. But if you start bumping against icebergs, or if you see seals and walruses swimming about, or if polar bears climb aboard with fearsome growls, then you have reached the Arctic regions, for all practical purposes.

So it is with alcoholism. As soon as the results of taking a drink (usually leading to a lot more drinks) become unsatisfactory, unpleasant, and unpredictable, you may be considered an alcoholic for all practical purposes. This is a loose interpretation of what constitutes alcoholism; it is meant to be that way. At that point your days of agreeable drinking are over forever. The only remedy for the sad situation is to put the cork in the bottle and leave it there. Too bad, but that's the way it is.

A Bit of Autobiography

One hot Monday morning in June, 1949, I awakened groaning. I had been drinking muscatel wine in large amounts since Friday night. I had excruciating pains in my bones and a number of other regions. I told my wife that I couldn't get up to go to work.

Her response was, "You have been drinking that stuff all weekend. No wonder you have horrible pains. I am going to get the A.A.s after you." And so she did. Some A.A. delegate called on Monday evening; but I don't remember much about him.

By Tuesday evening I was somewhat recovered, despite a few nips of the muscatel now and then. A couple of characters came around in an old car and conveyed me to a local closed meeting of A.A. It was a hot night. I had the sweats. Part of it was from the heat, part from what I had inside me.

I can still remember some of the people there. The main feature of the evening was a tape recording of a talk by Bill Wilson, the chief founder of A.A. I have foggy recollections of some voice going on and on. I got home that night and lapped up a few ounces of muscatel from the bottom of a half-gallon jug, then went to sleep. On Wednesday morning I was back at work, still somewhat shaky, with a cock-and-bull story that I had been having an attack of the flu. I didn't mention that the flu came out of a jug.

Up to then, I had been drinking something alcoholic nearly every day for several years. I had been getting mildly messed up to an increasing extent. I had a haunting feeling that perhaps I would need to stop someday, and the feeling was a most saddening one. By the time I was first brought in contact with the A.A., I figured that something needed to be done. So A.A. had the effect of changing me from a steady daily drinker into a periodic drinker with a short cycle! I would abstain completely for perhaps three or four days; then I would get a terrible craving, buy a bottle of something, usually wine, and absorb it all in one evening as discreetly and quietly as possible. Oftentimes I would wait until the family were asleep before I began my midnight potations.

In my brief nondrinking periods I attended various A.A. meetings and I derived a measure of benefit from them. This off-again, on-again pattern went on for several years. I had not reached the end of my alcoholic trail, but I was gradually getting there.

Alcoholics Anonymous (A.A.)

The most widespread effort to cope with alcoholism is that being made by Alcoholics Anonymous. Now, what is A.A. anyway? Well, it is a lot of different things. To start with, I shall give the official preamble, which is sometimes used to open A.A. meetings.

Alcoholics Anonymous is a fellowship of men and women who share their experience, strength, and hope with each other that they may solve their common problem and help others to recover from alcoholism. The only requirement for membership is a desire to stop drinking. There are no dues or fees for A.A. membership; we are self-supporting through our own contributions. A.A. is not allied with any sect, denomination, politics, organization, or institution; does not wish to engage in any controversy; neither endorses nor opposes any causes. Our primary purpose is to stay sober and help other alcoholics to achieve sobriety.

Note that interesting little sentence: "The only requirement for membership is a desire to stop drinking." In my opinion that is the crux of the situation. The same statement is made in A.A. Tradition No. 3 and in the Foreword of the Alcoholics Anonymous "big book." It means literally that anyone who ever had any trouble at all with alcohol, and wanted to stop drinking for as short a time as ten minutes, or even ten seconds, is eligible!

Note also that you do not, in theory at least, need to *call* yourself an alcoholic in order to belong to A.A. and attend the meetings. You can call yourself anything you want to. It is true that most persons giving a talk at A.A. meetings lead off by saying, "I am so-and-so, and I'm an alcoholic." This opening remark has some force of customary observance about it; but it is *not* obligatory.

So if any fanatic buttonholes you and asks you whether you *are* or *are not* an alcoholic, you can upset him nicely by repeating: "The only requirement for membership is a desire to stop drinking."

Most human institutions tend to drift slowly away from their theoretical principles; and A.A. is no exception. I have heard of persons in alcoholic trouble who tried to attend a closed meeting of A.A. but were repulsed because they were unwilling to utter the open-sesame phrase, "I am an alcoholic."

So I suggest, if you have any doubts, just utter the magic words and leave it at that. You may not be a full-fledged alcoholic yet, but if you are on the way you are likely to get there eventually. On the other hand, if you are just a snooper, I hope that the ferocious alcoholics who are having their anonymity invaded will give you the bum's rush or something equally drastic.

A.A. Open Meetings

An A.A. open meeting is open to anyone, whether he is alcoholic or nonalcoholic. Generally there is a leader and there are from two to four, usually three, other A.A. speakers. The leader opens and closes the meeting and introduces each speaker, who usually gives an account of his own drinking experiences and tells how he stopped drinking by means of A.A. and other methods. It is usual, whenever possible, to get in at least one woman alcoholic as a speaker. A collection is taken at some time during the meeting, which almost invariably closes with the Lord's Prayer. Afterward there is a social period with coffee, soft drinks, and food, and an opportunity for individual discussion or discussion in small informal groups.

As an introduction to A.A. the open meetings are very valuable and permit interested persons to hear a variety of alcoholic stories. When all goes well, some members of the audience who are uncertain about their alcoholic status may decide that they are alcoholics themselves and had better do something about it.

Unfortunately, some of the speakers tell such blood-and-thunder stories of their experiences, replete with all manner of horrendous detail, that mild or incipient alcoholics are repelled. These may feel that since they have not yet landed in several jails and hospitals, or have not yet lost their jobs and their families, they probably are not alcoholics. So many of them go away from the meeting and drink some more, and often get into serious difficulties before they finally quit.

Happily, the awful alcoholic autobiographies do not scare all such persons away or so disgust them that they want nothing to do with A.A. The horror tales do shake up certain moderately advanced drinkers so that they eventually stop drinking before their situations get too bad. In a few cases, the dreadful drinking descriptions are a source of intense fascination to mild, weak, guzzle-in-the-corner drinkers. Some of that variety apparently stop drinking and become loyal A.A. members so that they can associate with the two-fisted ex-drinkers and feel accepted by them.

Now, in theory the ideal would be to get at least one mild alcoholic to speak at each open meeting. If there was always at least one speaker to relate how he got just moderately messed up by alcohol, a lot of the mild and borderline cases would feel more identification and might be induced to discontinue their drinking before it got any worse.

In practice such an ideal is hard to attain. A lot of the mild drinkers are perhaps chagrined at not being worse than they are; at any rate, they feel diffident about coming forward and telling a rather colorless tale of drinking difficulties to a roomful of people.

But the bucket-of-blood boys! Many of them qualify as chronic and professional horror-mongers, ready to rush to almost any A.A. open meeting and put on their grisly show. The worst situation is where the speakers apparently get to competing, with each successive speaker trying to outdo his predecessor. I have attended several open meetings of this sort and I am convinced that the speakers on the whole did much more harm than good by alienating many in the audience without saying much of anything really constructive on how to throw off the alcohol habit.

Another criticism I have to make about open meetings is that most of the speakers tend to create an impression that A.A. is the one and only way to deal with alcoholism, that all the methods for arresting alcoholism are already known, and that A.A. is in full possession of them.

I dissent. That is one reason for this book.

A.A. Closed Meetings

A closed meeting of A.A. is limited to persons who consider that they are alcoholics or who have been sufficiently disturbed by alcohol so that they are possible or potential alcoholics. This limitation is in effect so that those present can speak freely without having nonalcoholics listening in; all those attending are either current drinkers or ex-drinkers. Closed meetings are of particular value in permitting newcomers and others to ask questions, discuss pertinent topics, and participate individually in the consideration of situations involving alcohol.

Most closed meetings have a leader, who is changed from one meeting to another. The meetings are relatively flexible in their operations. Usually the leader will tell his alcoholic history. Afterward, if there is time, the secretary or another person will make some announcement. There is a collection, and the meeting usually closes with the Lord's Prayer. The leader may be a member of the group, but perhaps more often he or she is from some other group, and has been invited to give a talk.

Sometimes a leader will take advantage of his temporary position, and of the politeness of his audience, to launch into a long-winded discourse on his alcoholic history, blow by blow, and even drink by drink. I have heard leaders talk for a full hour and a half about themselves and their battle with booze, leaving little time for discussion; indeed, the leader may get so wound up in his own eloquence that he even runs beyond the scheduled closing time. I have never been quite that bad myself, but occasionally I have become so windy that I was properly dusted off! After deep and lengthy cogitation I developed a better technique for leading closed meetings.

Probably the best over-all procedure for closed meetings is to hold the autobiographical material, if any, to fairly strict time limitations, not more than half an hour at most. This leaves time for questions and discussion. And if the discussion mainly concerns *methods* for dealing with alcoholism, then the meeting is likely to be of definite value to at least some of those present. Discussing ways and means for dealing with a personal alcoholic situation promises to be more fruitful than merely telling stories or ruminating about generalities and abstractions.

Furthermore, there are frequently a few persons present who are badly eaten up by some situation, question, or problem. It is a good thing to get them to sound off about their troubles and botherations. Oftentimes someone will have good suggestions on how to deal with a particular difficulty. To discuss specific situations troubling *specific* persons is an approach that usually yields something of value.

If the troubled souls can be induced to sing out their woes early in the evening, that is better than waiting until five minutes before closing time. However, many a heart-bowed-down will sit clammed up until quite late in the evening; then he will begin to unroll some colossal mess involving himself, his spouse, his children, his dog, his cat, his boss, and a horde of relatives too!

Such gigantic imbroglios can't be handled in five minutes. I don't even try to cope with them. If I am the leader, I put on a stern face and invite the bleeding hearts to drop in another time for more ample discussion. But if I am just a member of the group, or a visitor, and the discussion looks like an all-night performance, I fold my tent and steal away. After all, I need a certain amount of rest and sleep. I'll not get it if I sit around for hours trying to help untangle a mess that may take a year and a half to work out.

That is about enough on specific situations. To sum up: If they are brought out early in the meeting and in sufficient detail, helpful approaches can often be suggested. The more definite the situation, the more probable it is that something can be done about it. Long drawn-out discussions and arguments about

A.A. theory, principles, philosophy, and metaphysics are apt to be of less value. And if we get off into high-flown discussions about the good, the true, the beautiful, the infinite, and the eternal, we are likely to drift off into a gigantic fog-bank and just hang there. Fun maybe, but futile.

Are Special Types of A.A. Meetings Needed?

In addition to the two main types of A.A. meetings, open and closed, as already described, there are a few "open discussion" meetings here and there. These are run much like closed meetings except that members of the families of alcoholics and other interested persons may attend.

The three current types of meetings, valuable as they may be, perhaps do not do as good a job as they might. In particular, the general emphasis on stories, stories, stories, becomes tiresome after a time, at least to many persons. Different individuals have different emotional and intellectual needs and desires. They may get something out of the eternal round of autobiographies, but not so much as if there were more specific discussion of ways and means of dealing with alcoholism.

Perhaps in time some specialized forms of meetings will be developed. I know that this idea will curdle the blood of a lot of A.A. old-timers who are quite pleased and satisfied with things as they are. But since I fancy myself a great innovator, I am going to suggest some other types of meetings. They are only possibilities. They may work, or they may not; but if no one ever tries them, we'll never find out.

Why Not Try a Topic Meeting?

Many will no doubt regard this book as being mainly a mass of destructive criticism. But when alterations are being made on a building, destruction of some parts is necessary. I shall now proceed with something constructive.

Alcoholics Anonymous was originally derived from Buchmanism, which went in heavily for confessions of past misdeeds and high resolves to do better in the future. Perhaps this is part of the reason why so many alcoholic autobiographies are told, not only at open meetings, where they are suitable, but also at closed meetings, where they are less so.

In order to get away from lengthy stories and to try for more discussion of methods and ideas actually useful in dealing with alcoholism, one closed group that I know of dropped the stories almost entirely. Some meetings had no stories at all. Other meetings had short stories, in cases where some unusual character wandered in who might be interesting.

The principal procedure was to pause a few minutes before the end of each meeting to pick a topic for discussion the following week. In the intervening period, those who had attended the meeting were supposed to think about the topic to be discussed next time, so as to be able to boil up at the next meeting with all sorts of valuable and stimulating ideas. I don't know how many of them actually meditated on the topic between times, but the meetings were of unusual interest to those who were primarily interested in discussions.

In this meeting, no holds were barred. Party-line doctrines were not sacrosanct. No one got up and protested, "That's not A.A." The objective was to collect from all over the landscape any ideas and methods that might be of value to someone in dealing with his personal alcoholic situation.

Since a fairly wide range of outside ideas was encouraged, the discussions were usually lively, and at times even helpful! The meetings got violent a few times; but that is what a lot of the people wanted, and that is what they got. Of course, some others did not like the meeting and were even much upset. That is all right. Persons who are easily upset need a totally different type of meeting, and I'll suggest something for them in a moment.

For a topic meeting to hit all possible approaches to questions involving alcoholism, the greatest possible freedom of speech, opinion, and thought is desirable. A rather strong but fair-minded chairman is needed. If some organizer wants to found a group of this description, he now knows how to start it. I can recommend this kind of group for anyone who gets bored and jaded with the conventional A.A. closed meeting.

How to Have a Ferocious A.A. Meeting

As I have mentioned, it is helpful to certain persons to be able to hurl themselves around, roaring and screaming and howling out anything that pops into their active, even if somewhat disorganized, minds. That is why I long to see some bold, fierce innovator organize a sort of Kilkenny Cats A.A. group.

I know one or two groups whose closed meetings are an approach to this idea. Sometimes the opportunity to rip and roar is healthy for those present. They are filled with violent and disturbed emotions. To get them out in the open one way or another helps to keep the emotions from turning inward and eating the members up internally.

To make this kind of closed meeting effective, a lot of conventional A.A. ideas would have to be laid aside, at least for the duration of the meeting. It would be especially necessary to lay aside the notion that resentments are morally discreditable. I would advocate the fullest blowing off of resentments. Anyone who got moralistic about them would be penalized by having to put an extra quarter in the collection basket!

It would also be necessary to lay aside the prevailing A.A. notion that "you should never take another person's moral inventory." Most of us are somewhat blind to what is wrong with us until someone else opens our eyes. If I have a smudge of soot on the end of my nose, I won't know it unless somebody tells me. Then, if he does, I can of course get hopping mad and deny that the smudge is there. But sooner or later I am likely to look in a mirror, then wash off the offending smudge and be done with it.

It would also be necessary to lay aside the notion that all the answers to all alcoholic problems are already known and that

A.A. knows them all. It is seldom stated as baldly as I have put it, but it seems to be taken for granted by certain persons or groups. When that attitude prevails, a new idea doesn't have much of a chance. Some stick-in-the-mud, orthodox A.A. will probably pipe up with a mournful "That's *not* A.A." and try to kill the new idea on the spot.

It would also be necessary to lay aside the prevailing belief that all the troubles of alcoholics arise wholly and exclusively from their alcoholic addiction. Millions of people who hardly ever take a drink are plagued with much the same kinds of troubles that some of the alcoholics regard as being peculiar to themselves.

This business of releasing whatever disturbing thoughts are present is called "abreaction" by psychiatrists. A lot of it occurs in bars and taverns—alcoholic screaming and weeping about assorted troubles. But if a bit of sober abreaction can be pulled into at least a few A.A. meetings, that would undoubtedly help some people to some extent. Someone would at least occasionally come up with an answer. Here is a wonderful idea. What pioneer wants to give it a practice trial?

How About a Soothing A.A. Meeting?

A lot of A.A. members are shaky in their nervous systems, and easily upset, and hanging onto their sobriety by their fingernails. I think that these need some special sort of closed meeting designed to soothe and pacify them and in general to keep them from losing their balance. I must leave the details to somebody else, but if a proper effort is made, it would easily be possible to organize and run a closed meeting on a calm and level basis, with no one becoming much disturbed or upset about anything. I hope that somebody succeeds in this project. Undoubtedly it would be very helpful.

Holding an S.M.A. (Seldom Mention Alcohol) Meeting

Now I am coming up with something that is really going to shock certain A.A. stalwarts. I suggest that there could well be a special type of closed meeting designated as an S.M.A. (Seldom Mention Alcohol) meeting. I had this bright idea many years ago, but certain A.A.s shouted me down and nothing was ever done about it. Recently I heard the idea cropping up again independently; so here I go again.

A lot of us, either in A.A. or outside it, can't drink alcohol any more and we don't drink it. Having that firm conviction, a good many of us are disgusted, fed up, and bored with listening to those eternal talks about booze and the consumption of booze. We can't handle the stuff, we admit it, we intend to stay away from it. But why must we be harassed and tortured by blowhards who also can't drink but who make up for it by gassing about it all the time?

I might coin a very nasty aphorism to the effect that a good, standard, party-line A.A. member is a person who ruined the first half of his life by drinking too much and is ruining the last half by yapping about it at great and boresome length.

I have lately had some success in helping run a group of the S.M.A. type. Where it is, I'll not tell you. It is a great relief to be able to foregather with a few other alcoholics and not talk about booze *all* the time. If I said any more, the autobiography boys would pour in and ruin our nice little S.M.A. coterie completely!

Alcoholism as a Disease

Common doctrine in A.A. is to call alcoholism a disease and not a moral issue. However, the moralistic overtones and undertones involved in dealing with this so-called disease keep popping up, both in standard A.A. literature and in impromptu remarks of many A.A. members. This confusion between calling alcoholism one thing and then reacting to it and dealing with it as if it were another thing is fairly widespread and deep-rooted.

To get autobiographical again, this was the source of my first great bewilderment upon arriving on the A.A. scene. Speaker after speaker hooted and tooted, "Alcoholism is a disease, a disease!" But what did they do about this disease? They immediately launched into the old, familiar approach. The disease was going to be arrested by high moral resolves and efforts to lead a better life, strongly supplemented by religious (called spiritual) measures involving repentance of evil deeds, reliance on a Higher Power, prayer, and possibly small amounts of meditation and the like.

Having had some training in the medical sciences, I thought that this was a quaint way of dealing with an alleged disease. A few years previously (before my alcoholism developed) I had received some psychiatry for various emotional disturbances. It did not completely relieve me, but it helped. I eagerly sought for anything psychological in available A.A. doctrines—and found virtually nothing.

A common A.A. statement is that alcoholism is a threefold disease—physical, mental, and spiritual. The exact phrasing varies in different publications, but that is the gist of it. My criticism, either constructive or destructive, depending on how you look at it, is that in A.A. the "spiritual part of the program" is belabored to death while the physical and mental parts receive scanty, inadequate attention.

Over and over again we hear A.A. speakers assert that "A.A. is a spiritual program," as if that were a remark of the utmost sagacity and profundity. The trouble is that the word "spiritual" is an indefinite one. Consult a dictionary and you'll see what I mean. The word is simply hard to pin down to any definite meaning. On page 17 of the 1957 edition of the book *Alcoholics Anonymous Comes of Age,* there is a passing thought that anything spiritual is intermediate between the religious and the psychological. In any event, words of indefinite and shifting meaning tend to cause confusion.

To what extent A.A. is religious is another moot topic. Some A.A. publications say that it is, some say that it is not. Let no one try to controvert me; I have a lot of A.A. books at hand, and several folders full of pamphlets from various sources, and I am in a position to make a lot of direct quotations. But I don't want to. I only want to help develop A.A. in certain areas where it is needlessly weak.

Whatever a person's opinions may be in matters of religion or spirituality, it is at times possible to sense something in some A.A. members and some A.A. meetings that could be called spiritual. But it is something intangible, like the northern lights. It is not something that can be captured and taken home in a box or a bottle, or procured by the pound or yard. That intangible something is perhaps the best aspect of the "spiritual part of the program." It can sometimes be sensed or felt, but it cannot be confined or carried away in any tangible or material form, and in my opinion, it is not fixed or constant. Using that analogy of the northern lights again, it cannot be summoned but comes and goes regardless of anyone's wishes.

Away off at the other end of the scale, we find "the spiritual part of the program" at its very worst in attempts by various A.A. enthusiasts to trespass upon other people's religious views, perhaps by insisting that the twelve steps are mandatory steps and not suggested steps. This is another point on which the official and quasi-official A.A. literature is confused. We sometimes read that the twelve steps and similar doctrines are suggestions only. In other places we can read that implicit acceptance is very nearly obligatory or else all sorts of frightful things will happen to us!

If alcoholism can be regarded as a disease that attacks body, mind, and spirit (or soul), then it makes sense to go after the disease in all of its aspects and not merely harp on the spiritual aspects while neglecting the psychological and physiological aspects.

More Autobiography
(The D.T.s This Time!)

Long ago, when I was about ten years old, I read about delirium tremens in an old school text on the horrors of alcoholism. Many years later I heard a lot about the D.T.s at various A.A. meetings. I did not think it could happen to me; but on the other hand I did not think it could not happen. It was just an interesting bit of psychological data that I didn't connect with myself.

This was a period in my young life when I was sober by fits and starts and lapped up considerable amounts of alcohol in between my intervals of sobriety. Most of the trouble was inside me. I was in the midst of a neurotic conflict going on in my personality. Though I recognized that booze could cause me plenty of trouble, I just simply hated to give up the solace of the glorious golden juice! I kept trying vainly to recapture the days of long ago when alcohol temporarily dissolved my neuroses, so that I could sit around in a half-mulled condition feeling like the King of the Golden River, the Grand Panjandrum of the Infinite, or the Sublimest Mind of All Times.

The trouble was not *all* inside me. A certain part of it arose from the forms and sorts of A.A. that I encountered at that time. And it was just my hard luck that in A.A. circles I mainly happened to run into a lot of gloom-hounds and guilt-hounds who showed no outward signs of the mad joys of sobriety that they talked about. Anyway, I continued to drink, and some of my guzzling periods ran on for several days.

Now, in delirium tremens there are roughly two main forms: the form in which one has visual hallucinations, "sees things" (the famous pink elephants); and the form in which one has auditory hallucinations, "hears things." I happened to get the **rarer auditory form.**

It happened this way. After several days' drinking I was riding in the upper berth of a Pullman car, when a lot of little men hidden in the steel walls began singing scurrilous and slanderous songs about me. They did it in perfect time to the quakings and shakings of the train as it rolled along. I had never before heard a collection of rimesters and songsters who had such verbal ingenuity as this pack of miniature devils. Apparently they thought that I was a louse of the worst description—and they were letting me have it!

I don't remember what I did, if anything, to get the insulting trolls to stop their clamoring. I vaguely recollect that I tapped on the walls, but did not dare to tap very hard for fear of waking up the other occupants of the car.

I do remember distinctly that at this point my mind did a sort of split. The emotional part felt enraged and insulted and also upset and scared. But the intellectual part said in effect, "Well, at last you have the D.T.s. You have read about it, you have heard about it; and now what are you going to do about it?" Then I decided to try to remember the insulting songs the little men were singing so that I could do something about it later on. But after a while the songsters seemed to stop their tootlings and pipings, and a different sort of auditory hallucinations began to take place.

I heard people walking quietly in the corridor between the berths but distinctly making derogatory remarks about me. "That man in upper 9? He's looped, he's a mess, he's stewed to the gills." When I pulled open the curtains to confront my accusers, there was no one at all to be seen.

The train rolled on, carrying a collection of more or less restless sleepers and one juicy case of the auditory form of delirium tremens.

This experience frightened me, and I made further efforts to extend the time between drinking periods. I never got to the stage of visual hallucinations; I had no yen for a floor show of purple cockroaches dancing about. I am altruistic about it; someone else can have that type of entertainment.

Perfection Does Not Exist

Many alcoholics, or neurotics if you want to call them that, constantly search for perfection in one direction or another. This eternal chase after a will-o'-the-wisp makes plenty of trouble. If the perfectionist chases a whole pack of will-o'-the-wisps through some emotional swamp, the disappointment and frustration can be devastating.

In A.A. we hear, quite rightly, occasional criticisms of perfectionism and its attendant troubles. On the other hand we seldom hear any adverse criticism of attempts to be impeccable, to be morally and ethically perfect; in fact the tenor of A.A. doctrine as expounded by many speakers at meetings is that we *should* all try to become morally and ethically perfect. Even if we know that we can't make it, we should try.

It was just this sort of doctrine—that I should strive to be a paragon—that helped greatly to start me on the alcoholic trail. I was brought up to think that I should be ineffably noble. I could not achieve it. I felt like a worm. So I drank to kill the guilt feelings. That is not all of it, but it is a large part of it.

So now I don't care a bean any more about perfection of character. If I have a lot of big, black "defects of character," that is too bad. I am not going to try to rush out and slay them. All that I can do is to treat myself *reasonably* well and other people reasonably well. More on that later.

How Many Meetings?

Time after time we hear A.A. speakers say that the way to attain a contented and perhaps happy sobriety is to attend a great many meetings weekly. I have met persons who claimed that they had attended an A.A. meeting every night in the week for several weeks, on account of their extreme cravings for alcohol. For such cases, a heavy dosage of meetings may be desirable, especially if they are making their first real attempt to stop drinking.

For others, less frequent attendance may be better. Most persons have families, and the families would like them to stay home once in a while, or perhaps go out with them rather than make a mad dash to another A.A. meeting.

It is all an individual matter, and one need not feel sinful or guilty if his attendance is reduced to a sort of maintenance schedule—just enough to keep him sober.

I never force myself to go to an A.A. meeting just because someone tells me that I *should* attend. Sometimes I need extra rest and sleep. When I feel that way, I go to bed early. If my system is screaming for sleep, then sleep will do me more good than any A.A. meeting.

This means that I am just moderately active. I usually go to two or three meetings a week. I know by experience that certain meetings are likely to be helpful to me, and I attend those meetings rather frequently. Some other meetings are usually not helpful to me and I avoid such meetings; but occasionally I go back to them after an interval to see if they have changed. Sometimes a previously unsatisfactory meeting has developed into something good and helpful since I have been away from it. Or a meeting may be just about the same, or worse, and I then stay away from it.

Some unfortunate may wail that where he lives there is only one meeting a week, and that one is awful. That puts him right on the spot—and I can't do a thing about it. However, persons in areas where A.A. meetings don't help them are at liberty to organize meetings of their own. That will take a bit of effort, and of course the effort may fail. But it is better than just sitting back and crying that somebody else ought to correct the situation. And if worst comes to worst, they can simply associate with one or two A.A. friends without having a formal meeting.

No absolute rules apply. If it cannot be done one way, perhaps it can be done another way. The alcoholic must make an individual effort. The business of waiting around for somebody else to do something is a frequent source of disappointment—and relapses.

Thirteen Steps to Alcoholism

Before I go more deeply into my own views on alcoholism, I am glad to give some other points of view. Below are thirteen steps to alcoholism, based on those worked out by the National Council on Alcoholism.

1. You have begun to drink.
2. You start having "blackouts."
3. You find liquor means more to you than to others.
4. You consistently drink more than you mean to.
5. You start excusing yourself for drinking.
6. You start taking "eye openers."
7. You begin to drink alone.
8. You get "antisocial" when you drink.
9. You start going on benders.
10. You know deep remorse—and deeper resentment.
11. You feel deep, nameless anxiety.
12. You realize that drinking has you licked.
13. You get help or go under.

This is a fairly good description of what sometimes happens to *some* people who are developing into alcoholics. If you show some of the above signs and symptoms, you *may* be on the way to becoming a full-fledged alcoholic. Every case, however, is different.

It might be well to explain here what a blackout is. In simple language it is a condition in which a person takes in enough liquor so that later on, when he sobers up, he has no memory or recollection of what he did and what took place while he was under the influence of the liquor. In psychiatric language it is called "retrograde amnesia." These blackouts tend to occur relatively late in the development of alcoholism, not early as seems to be suggested by making them Step 2.

This is a useful list, but like most such lists it has weak spots that allow a person to get "picky" (just as I am doing right now!), enabling him to claim that he is *not* alcoholic because one or more of the symptoms don't appear in his case.

I don't know that drinking alone—presumably at home—is necessarily any more abnormal than drinking in company in bars, taverns, or restaurants. I once did most of my drinking alone, or perhaps with a few of the family around. It was a matter of expense. I would buy several bottles of beer, take them home, and lap them up by degrees. This was just after the repeal of prohibition. The depression was on and money was scarce. The same amount of beer served over the bar would have cost perhaps three times as much.

The benders mentioned in Step 9 are a little problematical. A good many persons go to conventions or off on vacations and sop up much more alcohol then they ordinarily drink. Then, when they get home again, they calm down and resume their former habits.

Anyone who must truthfully answer Yes to Steps 2 through 13 is very possibly on the road to alcoholism. Perhaps the basic question is not whether a particular phenomenon occurs in connection with your drinking, but whether the over-all results are so unpleasant that something definite needs to be done about it.

Signs of a Developing Alcoholic Disturbance

Here are thirty questions said to be used by Johns Hopkins Hospital in Baltimore in evaluating the development of alcoholism.

1. Do you require a drink the next morning?
2. Do you prefer (or like) to drink alone?
3. Do you lose time from work due to drinking?
4. Is your drinking harming your family in any way?
5. Do you crave a drink at a definite time daily?
6. Do you get the inner shakes unless you continue drinking?
7. Has drinking made you irritable?
8. Does drinking make you careless of your family's welfare?
9. Have you thought less of your husband or wife since drinking?
10. Has drinking changed your personality?
11. Does drinking cause you bodily complaints?
12. Does drinking cause you to have difficulty in sleeping?
13. Has drinking made you more impulsive?
14. Have you had less self-control since drinking?
15. Has your initiative decreased since drinking?
16. Has your ambition decreased since drinking?
17. Do you drink to obtain social ease?
18. Do you drink for self-encouragement or to relieve feelings of inadequacy?
19. Has your sexual potency suffered since drinking?
20. Do you show marked dislikes and hatreds since drinking?
21. Has your jealousy increased since drinking?
22. Do you show marked moodiness as a result of drinking?
23. Has your efficiency decreased since drinking?
24. Are you harder to get along with since drinking?

25. Do you turn to an inferior environment since drinking?
26. Is drinking endangering your health?
27. Is drinking affecting your peace of mind?
28. Is drinking jeopardizing your business?
29. Is drinking clouding your reputation?
30. Have you ever had a complete loss of memory while or after drinking? (A blackout.)

The way these thirty questions are usually presented, one Yes answer is supposed to warn that you may be an alcoholic. It is claimed that an answer of Yes to any two indicates that you are probably an alcoholic. And if you answer Yes to three or more, you are definitely supposed to be an alcoholic.

It is an interesting list and it has value, but I doubt if it is conclusive. My main objection is that it is a bit stacked, loaded, and tendentious. The difficulty always is to be sure that cause and effect are correctly related. It is not always certain that a change for the worse in a person's life, when he may be drinking, is due to the alcohol alone.

For example, Question 3: A lot of people lose time from work as a result of drinking—but they certainly do not all develop into full-fledged alcoholics. Question 16: A lot of people suffer a loss of ambition—perhaps with advancing years—but just how much of this loss can be attributed to drinking is an insoluble question. Question 17: A lot of people drink to obtain social ease, but that does not make alcoholics out of them.

So, theoretically, a person could be classed as an alcoholic on the basis of Yes answers to the three questions 3, 16, and 17. This may convince some people, but it does not convince me. I must have further evidence.

I am not opposed to the use of such lists, but since it is almost impossible to draw an exact line between social drinking and alcoholic drinking, I am not greatly impressed by such questionnaires, which at best have a limited value.

Total Abstinence the Only Remedy

People are fond of trying to make hard-and-fast distinctions; but in the world of reality one thing often blends into another with no sharp line of demarcation. An actual condition, however ill-defined, is more important than the label that somebody pins on it. And what is done about the condition is most important of all.

The question is not so much whether a person is "alcoholic" or "nonalcoholic" as whether or not that person finds alcohol so troublesome that he wants to stop drinking or decides that he must stop drinking.

Perhaps someone considers that he is only 10 per cent alcoholic. He can act accordingly. If he wants to avoid going the other 90 per cent of the way, it may be a good idea. Or if he prefers to keep on drinking so as to utilize his remaining alcoholic capacity, it is hard to stop him.

Perhaps someone else prefers to think that he is only "potentially" alcoholic. That is his opinion; and it may not be worthwhile for anyone to try to argue him out of it. He is entitled to go on drinking if he wants to; or, if he prefers, he can stop short—unless the habit has him in a bind. Then he is in real trouble.

No matter where you think you are on the scale, it is a fact that many people cannot drink alcohol with safety and satisfaction. They may get by with it on one, two, or three occasions but later on find themselves drinking uncontrollably. So in the end they may need to stop completely. The sooner that decision is made, the better.

How to Start Arresting Alcoholism

Many approaches to alcoholism exist, but the most widespread effort is being made by Alcoholics Anonymous. It is by no means a perfect effort. No human institution is perfect; and perhaps no such thing as perfection exists anyway. But A.A. is available in most parts of the United States, and persons who recognize that they may have an alcoholic disturbance are foolish if they do not at least give A.A. a try.

There are other efforts and movements about that deal with alcoholism on a somewhat different basis. I shall mention them later. They are, however, localized, while A.A. is far-flung indeed. For this reason A.A. merits first attention.

The initial procedure is of course to get in touch with A.A. In most places a local A.A. group is reasonably near at hand. Most likely it can be found listed in the telephone directory. If not, inquiry can be made of a local clergyman, doctor, lawyer, judge, or for that matter the policeman on the beat. In any event, if someone will ask around, A.A. assistance can probably be located.

If the alcoholic is too shaky or abashed to do it for himself, no doubt a member of the family or perhaps a neighbor will be glad to make the initial contact for him. Anyway, make contact!

Here I shall dissent from a theory that has been current in A.A. circles for many years, that the drunk himself must ask for A.A. help. If someone else does it, the results are supposed to be less satisfactory. There is a certain amount of truth in this idea but not too much. Certainly, if the alcoholic is willing or anxious to make contact with A.A., the initial results are likely to be better. But any number of persons (myself included) who had no particular enthusiasm for their first A.A. contact and were nevertheless more or less pushed into it, did eventually obtain benefit—perhaps after a long time. If no one will do anything at all, then nothing will get done. The active alcoholic will often have at least a limited degree of receptivity even if his active interest is close to zero.

After someone has gotten in touch, an A.A. representative (or more commonly two) is likely to call, possibly after a follow-up by phone. After that the wheels will begin to turn and something will happen. The visiting A.A. will no doubt have a talk with the active alcoholic. After that the alcoholic is likely to be convoyed to his first A.A. meeting, shaky and disrupted though he may be.

The Twenty-four Hour Plan

One of the most valuable and practical procedures used in A.A. to overcome alcoholism is the twenty-four-hour plan. Almost anyone can stop drinking alcohol for one day. So the neophyte A.A., or "pigeon," is commonly advised to try to stop drinking for just one day at a time, instead of taking the pledge for six months, or a year, or maybe for the rest of his life.

If a person can stop drinking for only one day, he may enjoy a definite feeling of accomplishment, even if he is shaking apart with the desire for a drink. Of course, he may slip and start drinking again; but he can then always try to abstain for another day and perhaps for a second day after that. Probably the best way is to try to gain periods in which no drinking is done, no matter how terrible the sufferer may feel. Thus the habit pattern of drinking every day can be broken up—rapidly by some, and more slowly by others.

Extreme alcoholics may have to stay sober for just a few minutes at a time, continually struggling to stay away from that first drink just a little longer until finally a complete day has gone by. I know something about it, because I finally had to do it somewhat that way. On the other hand, I knew a woman who stopped all at once and stayed stopped, despite the fact that she was a severe alcoholic and neurotic. She said that "it was just like turning off a faucet." So there you are. You never can tell what will happen; but unless you put forth some effort, nothing *good* will happen.

After the pattern of daily or almost daily drinking has been broken up, further procedures are up to the individual. Some A.A.s apparently operate twenty-four hours at a time all the rest of their lives; at least that is what some of them say. In other cases, once the habitual drinking is over, it ceases to be much of a problem, and the person abstains as a matter of habitual routine, without thinking at all about twenty-four-hour periods.

For periodic drinkers, special applications of the twenty-four-hour plan are required. They are persons who drink little if at all for many days, weeks, or months—then suddenly they are off on a drinking bout. Some of these bouts last for weeks; in others they are only one-night stands. Some periodics can go for a long time between bouts without even thinking of a drink. Other periodics do not drink at all for considerable periods but meanwhile are laying definite plans for going on a tear some time in the future.

In theory, when the periodic reaches the point at which one part of his personality is plotting and planning another good drunk, while another is fighting it, then he must really decide whether he wants to be drunk or sober. In the former unfortunate case, not much can be done unless someone can put him under restraint until the urge to drink has subsided again.

If the periodic himself recognizes that he is building up to a possible spree that he does not want, several things can be done. The conventional A.A. prescription is to go to a lot of meetings and talk to a lot of other A.A.s. Sometimes that works very well and the impulse passes off in time.

In other cases, supplementary measures may be needed. Medical, psychiatric, or spiritual help and guidance may be sought from those versed in such fields. This can sometimes be done by putting in a few days in a "rest home" that specializes in helping alcoholics. Such a spell away from work may be expensive, but usually will cost a lot less financially, physically, emotionally, and in every other way than yielding to the alcoholic temptation.

The A.A. Twelve Steps and How They Came About

Anyone who makes more than the slightest contact with A.A. is certain to hear a good deal about the Twelve Suggested Steps. They are supposed to be a general over-all guide for the rehabilitation of the alcoholic. Here they are:

1. We admitted we were powerless over alcohol—that our lives had become unmanageable.
2. Came to believe that a Power greater than ourselves could restore us to sanity.
3. Made a decision to turn our will and our lives over to the care of God, *as we understood Him.*
4. Made a searching and fearless moral inventory of ourselves.
5. Admitted to God, to ourselves, and to another human being the exact nature of our wrongs.
6. Were entirely ready to have God remove all these defects of character.
7. Humbly asked Him to remove our shortcomings.
8. Made a list of all persons we had harmed, and became willing to make amends to them all.
9. Made direct amends to such people wherever possible, except when to do so would injure them or others.
10. Continued to take personal inventory and when we were wrong promptly admitted it.
11. Sought through prayer and meditation to improve our conscious contact with God *as we understood Him,* praying only for knowledge of His will for us and the power to carry that out.
12. Having had a spiritual awakening as the result of these

steps, we tried to carry this message to alcoholics, and to practice these principles in all our affairs.

Some A.A. members make strong efforts to follow all these steps. Others attempt to follow only some of them. There is no absolute rule about it. In theory at least, individual A.A.s are entitled to take as little or as much as they want of the doctrine that they hear in A.A., since the only requirement for membership is a desire to stop drinking.

A bit of historical background on the twelve steps should be of interest. All kinds of unauthenticated stories can be heard at A.A. meetings; therefore I consider it desirable to give an account based on authorized A.A. publications.

Along about 1920 an American clergyman named Frank Buchman (1878–1961) founded an evangelistic movement called "A First-Century Christian Fellowship." Later, in England, it became known as "The Oxford Group," or sometimes merely "Buchmanism." About 1938, Dr. Buchman changed the name of his movement to "Moral Rearmament," under which name it continues to the present day.

The principles of the movement were based mainly on what came to be called the four absolutes: absolute honesty, absolute purity, absolute unselfishness, absolute love. The movement went in for house parties at which personal confessions were made and religious experiences were shared.

In 1934 or thereabouts an alcoholic named Ebby T—— was converted by the Buchmanites and thereafter was able to abstain for considerable periods. In one of his sober stretches, in the summer of 1934, he visited a friend, Bill Wilson. At that time Wilson was in Towns Hospital in New York City receiving treatment from Dr. W. D. Silkworth for inveterate and repeated alcoholism. The results of medical treatment had not been good, and Dr. Silkworth was inclined to regard Wilson as hopeless. The whole story is rather long, and for details it is best to read the original account in *Alcoholics Anonymous Comes of Age: A Brief History of A.A.* (Alcoholics Anonymous Publishing, Inc., New York, N. Y.).

Ebby told Bill that his improvement was based on an admission that he was licked and that he needed to take stock of himself and to confess his defects to some other person in confidence. There was also a necessity to make restitution for the harm done to others and to pray to whatever God there *might* be for the power to carry out these precepts.

During this period Bill Wilson didn't care much about God and was something of an agnostic. In December, 1934, after more drinking, he landed back in Towns Hospital. Ebby paid him a return visit and repeated what he had said before. After Ebby had gone, Wilson fell into a fit of depression and cried out to God to show Himself. The room "lit up with a great white light," and Wilson went into a state of ecstasy. He was startled by this experience and asked Dr. Silkworth whether he was hallucinating. Dr. Silkworth seems to have told him that he was not, but that some sort of "basic psychological or spiritual event" had taken place.

After a lot of further developments, Wilson, who had now stopped drinking entirely, was finally able to help a number of other alcoholics to stop drinking too. Finally, in 1938, it was decided to write a book about the new method of dealing with alcoholism. It later became the "A.A. big book" under the title *Alcoholics Anonymous.*

At about this time there existed two main A.A. centers. The one in Akron, Ohio, tended to follow the four absolutes of Buchmanism. The one in New York City tended to get away from the four absolutes. Meanwhile, between 1934 and 1938, a sort of word-of-mouth program more particularly adapted for dealing with alcoholism had developed. There are said to have been variations, but there were six steps, more or less as follows:

1. We admitted that we were licked, that we were powerless over alcohol.
2. We made a moral inventory of our defects or sins.
3. We confessed or shared our shortcomings with another person in confidence.

4. We made restitution to all those we had harmed by our drinking.
5. We tried to help other alcoholics, with no thought of reward in money or prestige.
6. We prayed to whatever God we thought there was for power to practice these precepts.

As the early A.A. slowly expanded and gained a few hundred adherents, it was decided to write a book explaining principles in order to win a larger following. One night in December, 1938, when the A.A. big book had progressed through about four chapters, Bill Wilson lay in bed with a pad of scratch paper on his knee. He had decided that the six steps needed to be more explicit, without a "single loophole through which the rationalizing alcoholic could wiggle out." Here I might just as well give a direct quotation from Bill Wilson in *Alcoholics Anonymous Comes of Age* (first edition, 1957, page 161):

> Finally I started to write. I set out to draft more than six steps; how many more I did not know. I relaxed and asked for guidance. With a speed that was astonishing, considering my jangling emotions, I completed the first draft. When I reached a stopping point, I numbered the new steps. They added up to twelve. Somehow this number seemed significant. Without any special rhyme or reason, I connected them with the twelve apostles. Feeling greatly relieved now, I commenced to reread the draft.

A couple of A.A. members dropped in on Bill, and he proceeded to read the twelve new steps to them. The visitors "reacted violently." There were objections to having "too much God in these steps." There were also objections to having the alcoholics "down on their knees" in Step 7 when asking God to remove all their shortcomings. Thereupon Bill "sprang to the defense of the new creation, every single word of it." After two hours of argument the three men took time out to drink coffee, and the initial debate subsided.

Some of the people in the Akron A.A. liked the new steps

very much, but in the New York A.A. there was violent debate about them. Material in Step 7 about praying on one's knees was deleted rather early. Step 12 originally spoke of a "spiritual experience." Since most A.A. members never had a sharp and definite spiritual crisis like Bill Wilson's, this term was changed after several years to "spiritual awakening." Except for this minor change, the steps remain as originally published in 1939.

Commentary on the Twelve Suggested Steps

In one of his essays Ralph Waldo Emerson says that "an institution is the lengthened shadow of one man." In a general way it is justifiable to say that A.A. is the lengthened shadow of Bill Wilson. In a specific way it is justifiable to say that the twelve suggested steps are likewise the lengthened shadow of Bill Wilson. When he wrote them, they no doubt applied strongly to his own case. According to his account, he wrote them all in about thirty minutes. Any later revisions appear to have been minor. I have heard talk at A.A. meetings that the twelve steps were developed by some mysterious conclave of scholars and spiritual leaders, but no evidence has been brought out to gainsay Bill Wilson's own words. He was undoubtedly influenced by other people, but the twelve steps as they stand are essentially his own creation.

Right here is where I become controversial. Forgive me if in my zeal I sometimes become repetitious. It seems to me that A.A. is filled with internal contradictions, at least as it is now operating. It is common doctrine in A.A. to say that alcoholism is a disease, but nowhere in the twelve steps do we find any specific or direct mention of the disease aspects of alcoholism except for Step 2, which speaks of a restoration to sanity. This might imply, though it does not say so definitely, that alcoholism is a mental disease.

Instead, the twelve steps place heavy emphasis on religious (or spiritual) and moral topics. Six of the steps deal with God, directly or indirectly. Seven of the steps deal with moral and ethical topics. For certain persons this is perfectly all right. Many alcoholics are adherents of various religions from which they derive their standards of conduct. If stopping drinking can somehow be tied in with their religious and moral views, the results for these persons are likely to be good. But many other alcoholics need physical and psychological treatment for their condition, and the twelve steps grievously neglect this aspect of the situation.

If the physical and psychological aspects of alcoholism can be adequately dealt with by other means, their omission from the twelve steps probably works no great harm. In other words, as long as the twelve suggested steps are not presented as a comprehensive cure-all, failure to emphasize the physical and psychological aspects of alcoholism may not be serious. Unfortunately, in many A.A. circles the twelve steps are *very definitely* regarded as a cure-all. I remember one character shouting at a meeting, "We have twelve tools in our repair kit and with them we can unscrew any nut who walks in that door!" It is seldom stated as crudely as that; but a good many A.A.s seem to feel that if they could somehow only "work the twelve steps perfectly," all their alcoholic (and other) troubles would be over and done with forever.

I'll stick my neck out again and say very definitely that the overemphasis of the twelve steps on moral and spiritual (religious) questions is a substantial deterrent to many alcoholics of heterodox religious views. Many have a rough time with the A.A. program. After hearing some preliminary statement that alcoholism is a disease and not a moral issue, they will usually get a harangue about the will of God, the grace of God, the power of prayer, and all the rest. As a result they are likely to think, rightly or wrongly, that someone is trying to impose some specific religious views on them. I have personally seen dozens of such cases, and there must be thousands more.

Of course, in strict theory (and I adhere to this theory), the twelve steps are *suggested* steps only, and not formally binding. On that basis a person can be a perfectly good A.A. just as long as he abstains from alcohol. In practice it does not always work that way. Many individual A.A.s as well as some A.A. groups tend to try to convert the suggested steps into mandatory or required steps. Usually the mandate is not a very rigorous one—lip service is often sufficient to quiet the enthusiasts—but it is often damaging to persons with painful principles that do not include verbal adherence to something that they cannot fully accept either intellectually or emotionally.

The twelve steps were worked up when A.A. was only about four years old. Most of the alcoholics who came in then were hard-bitten characters indeed, and had no doubt transgressed all sorts of moral and religious codes. Some twenty-five years later many of the new arrivals on the A.A. scene are relatively mild alcoholics, who have gotten into some trouble but have never done anything overwhelmingly bad. To me there appears little point in trying to harrow them up and to give them some awful "conviction of sin" over their guzzlings. Of course, a lot of people devoured by guilt feelings themselves like to manipulate others by stirring up guilt feelings in them, too. This, while understandable, does not necessarily help the new arrivals to stop their drinking.

I'll take my own stand on some of the later developments in A.A., not on the early twelve steps, which after all represent mainly the opinions of a single person. In particular I firmly support A.A. Tradition No. 3, which states simply and clearly that "the only requirement for A.A. membership is a desire to stop drinking." That certainly carries out the familiar A.A. slogan of "Keep it simple." Either Tradition Three means what it says or else it does not! Believing that it does, I'll take it as a starting point. The words of Tradition Three are also incorporated in the A.A. preamble, which too I regard as an excellent statement of principle. The Foreword of the big book *Alcoholics Anonymous* gives it a little differently: "The only requirement for membership is an honest desire to stop drinking."

I recommend that anyone who wishes to go deeper into the twelve suggested steps read that interesting book *Twelve Steps and Twelve Traditions,* a standard A.A. publication that is too often neglected. As to applying all twelve steps, I recommend it to anyone who can be so helped. There are many such. Others, if they prefer it that way, are entitled to follow whatever individual steps they find helpful and to leave the rest alone.

Steps 1 and 12 are the only ones that specifically mention alcoholism. Some persons follow those steps alone and call themselves "two-steppers"—and no one can show that they are any the worse for it.

Don't Get Hungry, Don't Get Thirsty, Don't Get Tired

Long years ago I heard a speaker an an A.A. meeting say, "Don't get hungry, don't get thirsty, don't get tired." I remembered his remark and was able to apply it to some extent, with rather good results. Then I kept hearing the phrase again, and applied it some more, with more good results. In brief, recognizing the fact that I was a physical organism, with physical requirements and physical limitations, was much more helpful to me than a lot of vague and lofty spiritual discussion.

Now, of course, the precepts mentioned can never be carried out completely. Few of us lead such sheltered lives that we are literally *never* hungry, thirsty, or tired. But any effort to minimize these conditions—any one of which can easily get us drinking again—can pay off handsomely indeed.

In other words, it is advisable always to bear in mind that we are flesh and blood, not disembodied spirits, and to act accordingly. If we cannot completely avoid hunger, and thirst, and fatigue, we can at least keep them within bounds. This may involve going at a much slower pace than we once did—but it is vital to many of us. Just how many alcoholics, over the years, have gone back to disastrous drinking as a result of letting themselves get all frazzled will never be known; but the number must be large. As for me, I just cannot drink any more; so I am taking no chances.

Three Possible Points

A commonly heard A.A. slogan is "keep it simple." Now, to make the whole vast topic of alcoholism very, very simple—in words, not in fact—I have boiled everything down to three possible points.

1. Learn how to live without alcohol.
2. Learn how to treat yourself reasonably well.
3. Learn how to treat other people reasonably well.

I offer these three points as possibilities only. They are not even suggestions. Anyone can do anything he wants to with them.

He can regard them as supplementary to the twelve suggested steps.

He can regard them as substitutes for the twelve suggested steps.

He can regard them as a special form of the golden rule—adapted for alcoholics.

Or he can regard them as no good at all!

In any event, the three possible points are likely to help a certain number of alcoholics or potential alcoholics for whom previous A.A. approaches and procedures did not seem to work.

There is one characteristic of the three possible points: they do not touch at all upon questions of religion, spirituality, or theology. All such questions are left entirely to the individual alcoholic. In many cases it may be preferable to operate that way. The three points simplify everything right down to basic elements.

Point 1 is essential, but it may not be enough unless emotional disturbances are eliminated that may push one back to the bottle.

That is where Point 2 comes in. A lot of people need to learn how to live with themselves. Elsewhere in this book I shall give off some possible approaches to that situation. It is a large order, and a number of things may need to be done.

Point 3 is also a large order. I have some suggestions to make on that one too—in fact, I have a slew of them.

The A.A. Slogans

Besides twelve suggested steps and twelve traditions, A.A. has some brief sayings known as slogans. These are often hung on the walls of A.A. meeting places. "Slogan" originally meant the war cry of Scottish Highland clans. We might regard the A.A. slogans as battle cries in a great crusade against the curse of drink.

In my opinion some of the A.A. slogans are the quintessence of applied wisdom. So far as I know, there is no list of "approved" A.A. slogans, but some of the more common ones are:

First things first.
Keep it simple.
Keep an open mind.
Easy does it.
Live and let live.
But for the grace of God.
Think.
This too shall pass.

The general attitude in A.A. at the time of my arrival on the scene in 1949 was that the twelve suggested steps were to be held in high esteem, while the slogans—at least some of them—were a bit corny. That was the impression that I got, which I don't insist was completely accurate.

I found that some of this "corn" consumed as a mental diet was distinctly beneficial. I could use the twelve steps only to a minor extent, but I could utilize most of the slogans a good deal of the time. I applied them as well as I could. By doing that (and a lot of other things too) I finally stopped drinking. In the process I found that I had to make up new slogans for myself. I passed some of them on to other people, and they were sometimes helpful and effective. This book contains a few of them.

Crawling around to A.A. meetings, I heard pithy comments by other people. A few such comments have also been incorporated in this book. If anyone wants to create a mild to moderate sensation at an A.A. meeting, he can dig up a new slogan from somewhere and hang it on the wall for other members to comment on. In fact, when things get dull, a slogan meeting might make a wholesome diversion.

Slips

In A.A. slang, when an alcoholic has been sober for a while, and then drinks again for either a short or a long period, he is said to have had a "slip."

It would of course be ideal if every alcoholic coming in contact with A.A. were to stop drinking immediately and stay stopped. Such an ideal result is not always attained. The clutches of alcohol are powerful, and it may be extremely difficult to break off sharply. Ingrained habits of many years are not easy to throw off and are exceptionally easy to resume. As someone has said, habits have a tendency to be very habitual!

At one end of the scale a certain number of persons come to A.A. and break off their drinking immediately, never to resume. They are the fortunate ones.

At the other end of the scale are those who attend A.A. meetings with great verve and violence. They listen to all the speakers. They read all the literature. They learn to mouth all the A.A. phrases as glibly as can be. But they do not stop drinking, at least not for long. In A.A. this sort of thing is called "bouncing." It may last for years. I ought to know; I bounced for seven years before I finally quit.

I have heard dozens of discussions in A.A. about slips, what causes them, and how to deal with them. It is plain, however, that if somebody slips and drinks again, the sooner he can be induced to stop, the better. And the more the new period of sobriety can be prolonged, the brighter are the chances for a permanent arrest of the alcoholism, regardless of what caused the slip.

We can no doubt get at *some* of the causes of slips. First

and foremost may be a person's feeling, or even conviction, that he is not "really" an alcoholic after all. Perhaps if he takes just one little drink—or maybe even two or three—why, this time he can control it. He has been to the A.A. and heard all sorts of stories—but of course those guys were dumb or perhaps they didn't have proper control, or will power, or something. And so another slip or spill is started.

Another frequent cause of slips is a mood of desperation or disgust, with some of that "Aw, what the hell!" attitude. Anything that can be done should be done to prevent the development of such mental states. Some go to an A.A. meeting; others go home and go to bed before the irritated feelings get the better of them.

An important cause of slips is the development of feelings of rage and indignation—the "resentments" that we hear a lot about in A.A. In resentment, there is a desire to pitch into someone. But a direct attack on the allegedly offending party may not be possible. So a jolly psychological mechanism sometimes called "retroflection" comes into the picture. A is mad at B. A would like to attack B, but is afraid to do so. The alternating feelings of rage and fear are pretty rough on A. So A turns his rage back upon himself—and attacks himself, as a convenient object, by pouring a lot of alcohol down the hatch. A peculiar emotional reaction? But a lot of alcoholic emotional reactions *are* peculiar. I shall deal with retroflection in more detail in another section.

I could ramble on. But, in a word, if a person has a desire or an impulse to drink, the best way to stifle it is to deal with the emotional forces pushing him towards the bottle.

Before ending this chapter, I am going to throw in another factor that probably causes a good many slips; namely, a desire to attract attention, and to hold the center of the stage. I have a strong impression that a certain number of persons go back to the bottle and get slopped because they know it will put them in the limelight, however hot and unpleasant the limelight may be.

Someone shows up at an A.A. meeting with a lot of alcoholic

troubles. The members rush to the newcomer with loads of advice and assistance. They give him discourses and harangues. They drag him to meetings. They do all kinds of things flattering to the ego of the pigeon.

Then, if the neophyte stops drinking, sooner or later he drops into the background and is just another A.A. He is enjoying the benefits of sobriety—but is no longer the great tragedian suffering and dying on stage. This may cause a comedown in his sense of self-importance.

It is hard to say just how such cases can best be handled. Some are best left alone for a while. It sounds like a hard thing to say, but if some—not all, but some—of these back-to-the-bottle boys are left to stew in their own alcoholic juices, they will rapidly or slowly tire of it all. Those who do not perish miserably *may* thereafter stop their guzzlings.

Keep It as Simple as You Can

In A.A. we frequently hear the slogan "Keep it simple," and I can agree with that exhortation in principle. However, talking about keeping it simple and doing so are quite different things. Nearly all members of the human race tend to talk one way and to act in another way—quite often in a way exactly opposite to what they say.

Alcoholism is frequently entangled with all sort of complications. There are emotional complications, family complications, religious complications, sex complications, and so on. The list is endless. And merely proclaiming that these entanglements are simple does not make them so.

Thus, at an A.A. closed meeting someone unwinds a regular snake-tangle of troubles and perplexities. Then what happens? Some cheerful chump puts on a big grin and announces in booming tones that the situation is really very simple, in direct contradiction to the actual facts. Oftentimes the only thing that is simple is the mentality of the know-it-all. Surely it is simple-minded to assert that something is simple when it is not. Noble and high-sounding words do not ease situations; in fact, they can complicate them even more.

The cheery guy may be grinning because things are going well for him and he is not in trouble at the moment. So, after declaring that everything is very simple, he probably goes ahead and tells the sufferer that he should do or ought to do all kinds of things that cannot be done—at least not then. The oughts and shoulds may involve all kinds of foggy moralistic and spiritual preachments that help the case in hand about as much as a sprinkling of rose-scented talcum powder helps a cancer. Again, fine words are no substitute for clear thought.

Stopping drinking is generally an easy operation on a short-term basis. The difficulty usually comes in staying stopped. In the presence of continuing complications that grind down a person's emotions and render him horribly miserable, or at least badly discouraged and confused, maintaining sobriety is a shaky and uncertain business. What is needed is to *start* taking action to deal with the difficulties. If some of these can be corrected, the victim will have a few rays of hope that the rest of his troubles can eventually be overcome. But without such hope, a return to the bottle is more than possible.

So probably the best thing is to try to buck up the sufferer into dealing with his difficulties bit by bit and little by little, a few things at a time. Thus a limited improvement may breed the hope of more improvement to come later. No rules can be made. Every case is different. But the big idea is to deal with the difficulties instead of ducking them.

Often it is a good plan to get a poor situation ended and done with—even if the way it is ended doesn't please us. I once owed a man several hundred dollars. We agreed verbally that I would pay off the debt at the rate of 10 per cent per month—which I did. When I thought that the debt was all paid off, lo and behold, the greedy fellow declared that an extra seventy dollars was due him. My previous dealings with him had been good; so this clipping was unexpected. Finally after some pulling back and forth, I had to pay him the extra seventy. I was sore about it, but I got over it. In a way it was worth the money to find that a formerly reliable person had developed into a money-grabber. I might have been clipped much more than seventy dollars. Incidentally, Mr. Grabber lost my business—and in the final analysis probably gypped himself more than he did me.

There are alcoholics who might be called "physiological alcoholics," who had no great emotional difficulties or soul-searing disturbances in their lives before they got into excessive drinking. Perhaps they slid into alcohol just because they liked to drink. Perhaps they figured that if a little was good, more was better.

Or maybe they merely fell into too much social drinking, or else they drank out of boredom. I am willing to guess that alcoholics of this description may find it easier to stop than those of us who had a lot of emotional difficulties long before we ever began to drink compulsively and excessively. For physiological alcoholics, it is likely to be much more a physical matter than an emotional and mental one. If they can stop before secondary involvements build up as a *result* of drinking, they should find it easier sailing thereafter. I imagine too, that such alcoholics will not find a great deal of value in this book. No harm done.

For most neurotic or emotional drinkers, the complications had set in well before the alcohol was poured over them. And when at last the alcohol is drained off, some of the miseries come with it; but these are mainly the later miseries that resulted more or less from the drinking itself. The primordial miseries that preceded the alcohol are apt to be there still. Unsuitable and ineffective patterns of reacting to things are not going to disappear automatically just because we are able to get dealcoholized. The primordial miseries may be even larger than before.

In a certain percentage of cases the emotional twists and disturbances can be handled by A.A. procedures already known and long practiced. In other cases they cannot, and a supplementary set of tools is needed. When the original A.A. big book was written, some A.A. members wanted a psychological book on alcoholism. They did not get it. The present book was written to start filling in this gap. I hope it moves someone to sit down and write the really comprehensive book on the psychology of alcoholism that is badly needed.

The R-A-G Emotions: Resentment, Anxiety, and Guilt

I am here going to deal with the disturbing emotions of resentment, anxiety, and guilt in a general way; in following sections I shall deal with them more or less individually.

In A.A. we hear a great deal about the horrors and undesirability of resentments. The emotion of resentment is regarded as a sort of major imp, attendant on the demon rum. Just how this came about I don't know for sure, but I've concocted a theory about it.

In brief outline I shall first give a general theory about resentment, anxiety, and guilt. It is only partly original. Some of it goes back to a Gestalt therapist whom I once consulted. What is Gestalt? Never mind now. If I have a chance, I'll come back to it.

The Gestalt psychiatrist pointed out that resentment and guilt are opposite aspects of the same thing. When we have a resentment, we think that someone has mistreated us and that he ought to feel guilty about it. When we have feelings of guilt, we think that we have done someone a wrong so that he is entitled to have feelings of resentment against us. Feelings of resentment or guilt, particularly guilt, are unpleasant. Whether the feelings have a solid basis in fact or are only perched on some illusion or delusion, they make people feel so very uncomfortable that they go through all sorts of mental contortions trying to avoid them.

Those who have been around A.A. quite a bit have heard resentments denounced in stirring tones time and time again. So perhaps after a while they begin to feel *guilty* about their resentment feelings. This creates a juicy emotional and psychological jumble. Formerly they rather enjoyed their resentments, but now they feel vile and wicked about having them. They try to get rid of the resentments but don't know how to do it effectively.

If they don't feel guilty about having resentments, then they often feel guilty about their past alcoholic misconduct. They struggle hard against their guilt feelings—but, again, they don't know how to deal with them. Oftentimes they just try to crush them out of existence.

Both resentment and guilt are fairly definite feelings attached to something that happened in the past or is happening currently. These definite feelings can be talked away, or denied, or swept under the rug—to some extent. But that is likely to create anxiety. There are probably several different kinds of anxiety, which is just another name for nervousness. Right now I am dealing with only one kind, the form of anxiety that comes from attempts to deny guilt and resentment.

We can call it the R-A-G setup of resentment, anxiety, and guilt. That is easy to remember; if these emotions, any of them, get out of hand, they can reduce you to a "rag" emotionally.

Resentment and guilt, then, are usually attached to something definite. And when one tries to crush them out of existence and deny them, they are likely to come back in the form of anxiety. By refusing to deal with unpleasant emotions attached to something definite, the result is an anxiety that is often very indefinite. People have a vague and horrible feeling of unease. They are badly scared, but they don't know what they are scared of. Perhaps the anxiety takes the form of a feeling of impending doom. Sometimes people say that they feel that things are "closing in on them." So as a result of refusal to admit to definite unpleasant emotions, they get something that is considerably worse on account of its very indefiniteness.

Resentment

Now for some comments on resentments. My guess is that resentment was the most conspicuous emotion in the first few hundred A.A. members. Probably a good many of them were exceedingly violent in both words and deeds, and tended to rant and rave at great length about all the wrongs that had been done to them. So perhaps resentments attracted early attention in A.A. on account of their ubiquity and conspicuousness.

As I have said, resentment is a violent and unpleasant emotion directed outward. Someone feels that he has been wronged; accordingly he wants to wreak vengeance on whoever has wronged him. Despite the low esteem in which resentment is held in A.A., I still consider that—on a purely biological basis—it is one of the "healthier" unpleasant emotions. It is potentially directed toward some sort of *action,* even if the action is ill-advised. One animal attacks another; the animal attacked comes back at his aggressor with tooth and claw. One ape man swings at another with a big club; so the anthropoid under attack slams a rock at the character with the club. One drunk "insults" another drunk, and the insultee takes a poke at the offender.

As far as I can make out, resentments are the one and only cause of barroom brawls. When and if active alcoholics get into A.A. and stop drinking, they generally get their more violent emotions under somewhat better control. But not always! The old reaction patterns persist. The dried-out drunks still tend to react in the same way as before when their emotions get worked up. Most of the resentments persisting are vented in the form of violent verbal assaults. I have seen instances of fisticuffs at A.A. meetings; but such things are rare.

The reason is that in a moderately civilized and polite society, physical attacks are regarded as primitive and antisocial. Many of the bystanders become upset when slugging begins! So often they try to separate the battling contestants. In any event they are apt to be unsparing in their condemnation of such conduct. They berate and revile the battlers by telling them that their actions are discreditable. They try—perhaps unconsciously—to convert the rage and resentment feelings of the contestants into shame and guilt. R-A-G! Here it comes again!

Of course the potential physical battles seldom get beyond the jawing, arguing, and threatening stage. Words tend to be substituted for action in many human affairs, and in some cases such a substitution may be beneficial. But if the resentment feelings are transformed into guilt, or worse yet, into a nebulous anxiety, the chances of resumed drinking are somewhat increased. It is just my guess—no more than that—that a resentment which is in some way expressed is less likely to cause drinking than are crushing and crushed-down anxiety and guilt feelings.

Guilt

Someone will think that after commenting on resentment, we should next go on to anxiety. However, anxiety is mainly the result of the polar opposites of resentment and guilt, so that it is more logical to consider anxiety last in the R-A-G trio.

Guilt feelings produce much less social condemnation than resentment feelings. For one thing, the unpleasant feelings are directed inward, and the guilt-ridden person seems to be no menace to others. The poor guy is busy attacking himself and is not likely to attack others. In extreme cases he may commit suicide, but that is another matter.

Another reason why guilt feelings arouse little general objection is that those who feel guilty are much easier to manipulate than those who feel resentful. The guilt-ridden person feels low and contemptible. One part of him—the conscience, which roughly corresponds to the Freudian superego—is busy cursing, condemning, and sitting in moral judgment on the rest of him. He feels badly already; and he can often be made to feel a whole lot worse by stirring up, or stimulating, or otherwise intensifying, the already existent guilt feelings.

In fact, first generating and then playing upon guilt feelings is one of the most effective devices by which institutions and individuals control and manipulate people. Sometimes it is done for more or less "worthy" ends; but in other cases the worthiness of the ends is questionable indeed.

I shall give some examples of mild and not-so-mild forms of manipulation by implanting and nurturing guilt feelings. If you attend college, the professors are likely to lecture you on how hard you ought to study. If they tell you that it is for your own good, that is reasonable. But if they tell you that it is necessary in order to be a credit to dear old Alma Mater, that is less reasonable. And if they try to scare you, that is even less reasonable. Perhaps they are only trying to hang up a group performance that will redound to their own credit.

Meanwhile, the athletic coaches will put on a much stronger act. They will bark and bellow at you to try out for some team—if they think that you are suitable "material" to be manipulated. Perhaps you are actually inclined to do some studying for your own benefit—but never mind that! The coaches and the sports enthusiasts will spout long tirades about how crucially important it is to defeat various hated rivals in competition. So after listening to a lot of such stuff, perhaps you try out for the football team—impelled by feelings of guilt that you are a mouse and not a red-blooded he-man. Of course, if you *want* to play football, that's a different matter: then you have reasonable motivation and are not merely a manipulated puppet.

If, at the very least, you don't try out for the chess team, you are apt to feel pretty guilty about it all. Still, you will not be left to sit in a corner nursing your sense of unworthiness. The rah-rah element will breathe fire against the seat of your pants to persuade you that you ought to pay your way into a lot of sports events and sit in the stands cheering loudly. If you don't, then a motley collection of cusses will tell you that you are a miserable worm, totally lacking in the old school spirit.

Well, let us assume that you finally graduate from dear old Hot Rod College. Is that the end of it? Not on your life! Next the Alumni Association will get you on their mailing list and will keep you there until you are known to be very dead indeed. They will pursue and pester you forever more with tear-jerking appeals for money. If you don't cough up, they'll try to make you feel guilty; and if you do cough up, then they will shortly be back after more money, plucking and playing on the old guilt strings.

And now, on to the touchy field of religion. In theory, religious institutions are supposed to guide their followers toward a better and a nobler life, and to a considerable extent most of them do function that way. On the other hand, many of them tend to operate as guilt-producing machines. If they were to concentrate on preventing misconduct that is clearly and demonstrably evil and productive of suffering and misery, efforts to deal with such forms of misconduct by promoting guilt feelings might be justified.

Often, however, people are made to feel guilty over mere thoughts, ideas, and feelings that are *not* carried out in action to anybody's harm. Worse than that, various real or alleged sins are defined so vaguely, or in such a broad and sweeping fashion, that if the churchly preachments were taken literally, no one at all could escape tremendous guilt feelings.

In any event, many people gradually accumulate guilt feelings over one thing or another (which may or may not be of real importance). The accumulated guilt feelings are more or less discharged by attending church, by contributing money, or by some other religious activity. The sense of partial or total release from guilt feelings gradually evaporates. Then people start feeling unworthy and guilty again. And perhaps the feelings are alleviated once more by some form of religious activity. This process can continue indefinitely.

Personally, I don't think too highly of this kind of religion. In the final analysis, there is probably not much sense in lamenting one's past misconduct and reviling oneself for it. Probably it is much better to take measures to prevent such misdeeds in the future. I once was haunted with corrosive guilt feelings, but most of the things that I felt guilty about did not amount to much anyway. I got rid of the unreasonable guilt feelings by means of several brands of psychology and psychiatry which demonstrated that my guilt feelings made no sense. That left a certain residue of actual past misdeeds. When finally I was able to see that there was no reason to expect that I *should* be able to handle every situation perfectly, then the genuine guilt feelings eased off a great deal also. I was able to look back on past misconduct with proper regret, but the ghastly feelings of shame, blame, guilt, and remorse dwindled to small proportions.

There are plenty of other guilt-mongers around. There are the numerous charities, eternally howling for more and more money. I can handle *them* all right! There are just a few causes that I regard as great and noble, and sometimes I toss them a few shekels. I let all the rest go slam! The world has always been full of evils that in my opinion will still be around for thousands of years after I am dead and gone. H. L. Mencken, the late sage of Baltimore, wrote that "human society is full of incurable ills, just as the human body is full of incurable malaises." This may seem to be a gloomy point of view; but I think there is a lot of truth in it.

That about winds up the subject of guilt for a while. In closing, I might say that a sensible sense of guilt is necessary and desirable. It is desirable for all of us to have enough conscience, or superego, so that we can avoid the guilt feelings attached to rape, robbery, murder, and similar excesses *in advance* of committing such crimes.

The sense of guilt that arises from vague and confused feelings that we somehow owe a great debt to society, I don't favor. You have to be reasonably cooperative with the rest of the world; but if you allow someone else to serve as your conscience, your life will be miserable indeed. This is because the desires and demands of others—the rest of the human race considered collectively—are utterly without limit. I am looking out for myself. I don't want to harm anyone else in the process, but people who come howling around with a lot of excessive demands are likely to get short shift from me.

Anxiety

Anxiety can arise from almost any feeling that a person has but does not want to recognize. A classical Freudian example is the anxiety resulting from sexual feelings that the individual regards as deplorable or unworthy. Attempts to escape from other undesired emotions and feelings can also lead to anxiety. For example, I think that much anxiety among alcoholics results from attempts to avoid resentment and guilt feelings. That is why I put that kind of anxiety right in the middle of the R-A-G trilogy.

If anxiety arises from an emotion that is crushed out of existence or repressed, then it might arise from *any* emotion, pleasant or unpleasant, that one does not want to accept or recognize. For example, a person might feel disgusted at being expected to eat some kind of food that he does not want. But if he has been indoctrinated with the idea that it is not mannerly to feel disgust under such conditions, then he is likely to recognize only a feeling of anxiety or nervousness.

If a girl hears a lively dance tune, she may feel like dancing; but if she has been brought up to think that dancing is wicked, she may crush her transitory feeling of pleasure at the tune and develop some kind of anxiety attack instead. In fact she might "rationalize" her anxiety by saying that she was tempted by Satan to dance—but overcame the temptation at the cost of feeling considerably rattled about it.

Back to alcoholism. A devoted A.A. has a lot of resentments. But he has heard at many meetings that resentments are *awful*. Therefore he thinks he should not have any resentments. So he keeps them crushed down and refuses to recognize them. As a result he gets nervous, edgy, jittery—in a word, anxious. Too bad.

This sort of thing results from the noble "sediment" uttered in pious tones: "We alcoholics can't afford to have resentments!" Okay, brother, roll your eyes and talk all you want to about the feelings that you can't "afford" to have. Maybe you can't afford to pay the taxes on your house, but if you don't pay up somehow, rough things will happen to you!

Windup on the R-A-G Emotions

I'd like to make it clear that in proposing some helpful approaches to the odious R-A-G emotions of resentment, anxiety, and guilt, I am giving my opinions only, based largely on personal experience and on observation of other alcoholics. My comments are only a first approximation to an attempt to deal with the situation.

Now that we have a tentative theory about the R-A-G emotions, what can we do about them? A number of things can be done. The first thing is to recognize that these emotions actually exist in us. The second is to face the emotions and deal with them instead of brushing them away and making out that they do not exist. The third is to analyze the emotions and decide how far they are justified. The fourth is to take effective action against the disturbing emotions.

Many people seem to think that they never *should* have any unpleasant feelings. This should feeling may be directed either inward or outward. Perhaps I should be in such marvelous control of my life that I never feel disturbed about anything; if so, it is the A.A. doctrine about the desirability of "serenity" carried to a nonsensical extreme. To expect me or anybody else never to feel disturbed about anything is a large order indeed. I don't think it can be done on that basis. But I do think that it is possible for most of us to gain somewhat more serenity than we now have or have had in times past.

When the should is directed outward, it amounts to a claim or demand on the rest of the world that it should reorganize itself to please us, and suit us, and satisfy us. That is an even larger order than the same feeling directed inward. After all, other people are busy looking out for themselves. Many of them are emotionally disturbed; so it is not surprising if some of their performances are pretty irritating. In A.A. we sometimes hear the remark, "You can't change other people." That is not entirely true, but it is largely true. You can change other people to some extent, but it may take extreme measures to do so. And of course there is not much chance of a single person changing the conduct of all his associates en masse; so he might consider making some changes in himself instead.

These oughts and shoulds, whether directed inward or outward, make millions of people uncomfortable indeed. For many alcoholics the results are extra bad. A great many become alcoholics because they think it an outrage whenever they feel uncomfortable or even mildly perturbed about anything. So they down a drink, with the usual end results. Refusal to endure even mild discomfort causes millions to take sedatives and tranquilizers. It is impossible to lead a life devoid of all unpleasant emotions; but by suitable measures most of us can trim down unpleasant emotions to such a low level that at times existence is quite tolerable or even pleasant.

Before I finish this windup on R-A-G, I have another comment to make. It is curious that seven of the A.A. twelve steps (numbers four through ten) deal more or less with guilt feelings, at least by implication. Not one of the twelve says anything clear or definite about resentments; perhaps they may be assumed to be lurking somewhere in the background. It's an interesting point. Perhaps someone "should" clarify it.

As to the "moral inventory" of Step 4, I don't call it that. I prefer to call it a personal appraisal or psychological appraisal. As to the "defects of character" mentioned in Step 6, I came to recognize through psychotherapy that many times in my life I had acted in a way that was dumb, disagreeable, and discreditable. While I had plenty of personality quirks, still I was rather short on big, black defects of character. In going over my life, I found that I had been the victim far more often than I had played the villain. If I had been more of a villain and less of a victim, my life would have been much more agreeable. As a matter of fact, I found that I had never been as bad as I wanted to be! It would have been pleasant to live a life of delightful wickedness like the fictional Dr. Fu Manchu, but it's too late now and nothing can be done about it.

Three Mental Mechanisms: R-I-P

I have given off three possible points for a super-simple approach to alcoholism and I have commented on the three ghastly R-A-G emotions. Now I shall consider three mental mechanisms—three emotional stunts or twists that are common to most of us and that get us all into trouble at one time or another. My discourse is mainly adapted from the Gestalt therapy of Dr. Fritz Perls. (See *Gestalt Therapy*, by F. S. Perls, R. H. Hefferline, and P. Goodman; New York: Julian Press, Inc., 1951.) The basic ideas are those of Dr. Perls, modified from earlier Freudian theories. I have jazzed them up and jollied them up a bit to adapt them to our battle against booze.

By name the three mechanisms are Retroflection, Introjection, and Projection. R-I-P does *not* stand for "rest in peace"! Instead it might stand for Ripped in Pieces, for if these three mechanisms get out of hand, that is what will happen to you emotionally. You are likely to get a severe neurosis. In very extreme cases, you may develop a neat psychosis, and that would be undesirable since it would take you out of circulation for a long time, perhaps permanently.

If you will read over the following material on the R-I-P mechanisms and then reread and reread it, after a time you will catch on to the basic idea of how these mechanisms work. When that happens, you may be able to deal with them by methods given elsewhere in this volume.

Retroflection

I quote directly from Dr. Perls: "Retroflection means that some function which originally is directed from the individual towards the world, changes its direction and is bent back toward the originator."

Retroflection may take all kinds of forms. Thus, if a person talks to himself, it is in lieu of talking to someone else. There is a kind of split in the person's makeup: one part of him is lecturing, or berating, or perhaps consoling, another part. This is a mild and perhaps a normal form of retroflection.

The really rough kind comes when a person has aggressive impulses against someone else (those terrible resentments) and would like to attack him in some fashion. But if no external attack can be made, then the resentful person will proceed to attack himself.

Thus, if someone falls deeply in love but is frustrated or disappointed, the previous feeling of love may be turned into hate, at least in part. The aggrieved person then feels mixed love and hate toward the former beloved. The hate component leads to a strong wish to punish the one who has thus blighted a loving heart! If it builds up and up, the hatred may lead to a desire to kill the one who has caused such cruel disappointment. Murder may be the result. But rather more often suicide, real or pretended, may take place. The disappointed person, wanting to kill the other party but unable to do so, will substitute himself and thus gain an irrational emotional release.

A classical case of retroflection appears to be Job in the Bible story. Poor Job had all sorts of afflictions. Part of the time he blamed God for them. Then apparently he got scared and feared that God would punish him even more; so he shifted around and took a conventional religious line toward God. But he put in a good deal of time sitting on a dungheap, tearing his hair and picking at his skin and generally attacking *himself*. Apparently when he got really wrought up, he wanted to attack God for afflicting him so, but since he could not do it he obtained partial emotional relief by mistreating himself.

Well, now, how does retroflection apply to alcoholism? That's an easy question to answer. Alcoholics who rush out and get drunk because they are mad at someone else are indulging in retroflection. They can't attack the other party; so they attack themselves. So the next time my gentle reader gets howling mad and turns into my ungentle reader, filled with hellish resentments, please remember my words on the subect of retroflection. I don't know that a theoretical knowledge of the mechanism of retroflection will stop any great number of alcoholics from going out and getting tanked up the next time they become enraged at somebody. But if some knowledge of retroflection gets around in the more intelligent circles of A.A. (and elsewhere), it may serve to prevent at least some bouts of retroflective rage drinking. Every bit helps.

The next time you get riled up about something and want to grab for a bottle of something, you may be seeking to blot out an unpleasant situation. Or you may want to attack someone whom you cannot attack. The remedy is to stop and analyze the situation to see if it actually merits such an outburst.

Attempts to suppress or repress resentments—the "get thee behind me, Satan" approach—are likely to fail in the end. There is a Freudian doctrine about "the return of the repressed" that has a great deal of validity. Emotions that are crushed down are almost sure to return, most likely in a changed form as nervousness or anxiety—a good thing to remember.

Introjection

In the R-I-P mental mechanisms, retroflection was best handled first because it is the most violent of the lot, involving an attack of some sort on oneself. Introjection is a more passive kind of mechanism: for our purpose it is the process of taking something into your mental and emotional makeup without really absorbing it and assimilating it. To give an analogy, if you swallowed some pebbles, you certainly could not digest and metabolize them. If you did not vomit them up or pass them on and they remained in your system, they would certainly lie heavy on your stomach and make you very uncomfortable. For another analogy, if you run a splinter into your finger, it remains a foreign body and a source of irritation until you pull it out.

Introjection means taking in some opinion, viewpoint, doctrine, or belief that does not suit your personality. Usually the item that you introjected was pushed onto you or pushed into you by someone in authority who "took advantage" of your weakness to indoctrinate you.

Most of us have been indoctrinated by parents, teachers, relatives, associates, and others when we were small children and unable to resist effectively. Nevertheless, the process can also go on in adult life. Churches, schools, government organizations, and even A.A. (or at least some of its members) can pressure us into introjecting unsuitable material.

To give a food analogy again, suppose that little Johnny has a nervous mother who is filled with irrational neurotic fears that Johnny won't grow fast enough. So what does Mother do? She stuffs little Johnny. She browbeats him into engulfing great wads of spinach washed down with enormous slugs of milk. Then, on top of that, Johnny is forced to eat meat, potatoes, and other things. If Johnny is able to, he will hold it all down and eventually it will work through his system. But if normal peristalsis and all that does not take place, young Johnny will hold it down as long as possible (maybe from fear of being punished). But at last an outraged physiology will assert itself, and Johnny will "up-chuck" the whole load. I am painting a grim picture—but I have seen it happen.

And something similar will happen to you, Mr. Reader, or Mrs. Reader, or Miss Reader, if you try to assimilate what does not suit your particular mental metabolism. You will get mental indigestion. Millions suffer from this dismal condition. They have taken in a lot of stuff that does not suit them, but, largely through fear, they don't care or dare to get rid of it.

So perhaps it is best if you take in only the parts of this book that seem to fit your case. I am not on hand to tell you what to do or how to do it. Maybe you really need to take in something that you don't want to in order to make up for some great lack in your makeup; however, most such cases are best handled by professional psychotherapy.

There are many methods for dealing with alcoholism. I can touch on only a few of them. My own approach is A.A.—plus a large amount of additional psychotherapy of a sort not commonly found in A.A. at this writing. Within A.A. itself there are numerous variations in approach. Perhaps there are as many forms of A.A. as there are individuals in A.A.

In a very general way, the two extremes of the A.A. spectrum might be called the "no musts" school of thought, and the "accept and do everything" school. The "no musts" people are fond of giving off the aphorism, "There are no musts in A.A." Well, I must differ from that point of view. Perhaps I can take a stand on a "one-must" outlook. That one is pretty simple. You must stop drinking alcohol sooner or later; otherwise the deplorable things that have happened to you already will be followed by even worse things next week, next month, or next year.

Now, getting really violent this time, I am going to throw some hot shot and cannon balls into the "accept and do everything" element. In the first place, it simply is not possible to accept and do everything encountered in A.A. Too much of the advice is contradictory. And if you let them, the "do everything" people will load you down so excessively that being in A.A. is likely to turn into a burden instead of a benefit.

I have heard speakers claim that in A.A. they did everything they were asked to do. Maybe they are sincere; but I have certain doubts. I once made an attempt to do a lot of the things—not all but a lot—that I was asked to do. As a result, the A.A. promoters and organizers ran me ragged. Besides attending local meetings when I really needed sleep, I allowed myself to be dragged off on long trips to speak here, there, and everywhere. This was noble of me, but it was not bright. I became more and more fatigued, got disgusted with A.A. and all its works, and—you've guessed it—back to the bottle I went for considerable stretches. When I finally quit for good, I followed a more restrained pattern. No longer did I let the hullabaloosters "introject" me with performances that they were interested in while I was not. I went to A.A. meetings that seemed to be helpful *to me* and let the others go.

I could holler away till the nineteenth of May about the horrors of introjecting things that don't suit. Instead I'll only holler a little while longer and then quit. Some A.A. groups seem to have a custom of pressuring newer members to give a talk after they have been sober for a while; three months seems to be the usual period. Maybe it is helpful and maybe it is not; but I am willing to guess that at least some of those introjected with the idea that they *must* speak develop resentments or anxiety and perhaps even get drunk over what they consider coercion.

Perhaps the most common introjection trouble consists in trying to introject the twelve steps even when they are out of line with one's views on spirituality and religion. I have seen a lot of this. In my opinion pressure to introject the twelve steps—or any other doctrine—usually does more harm than good. There are a fair number of atheists and agnostics in A.A. Assuming that they are staying sober on the basis of their atheism or agnosticism, I see no reason why they should be pressured into giving even lip service to something that they find unpalatable. In addition the world is full of people who are simply nonspiritual and nonreligious. Some of them are alcoholics. If they can get off the booze without going into the spiritual field, I don't see why anyone has the right to harass them to get them to do things differently.

Lastly, there are a lot of people around who are totally nonpsychological. The psychological stuff leaves them cold. Accordingly, they would be ill-advised on reading this book to try to ram it into their makeup willy-nilly. If they don't like it, they can leave it alone and no one is harmed at all.

Projection

Now we come to the last member of the R-I-P trio. Projection consists in having inside you a disturbing emotion or feeling that you do not want to accept. Since, however, the feeling is coming from somewhere, and you cannot accept it as your own, it is very easy to imagine that it is coming from somewhere outside. Someone else has the emotion (so you think). You have projected it outside you!

A classical case often mentioned in the psychology textbooks is the not-too-attractive and not-too-young unmarried woman who is bothered by sexual thoughts. What the poor woman wants is some sex activity and satisfaction. However, she was brought up to think that sex (at least in her circumstances) is pretty terrible. Also, she can't get any anyway! Unable to face the fact that she is feeling both sexy and frustrated, she keeps brushing the disturbing thoughts away, but they keep coming back in one form or other.

Since the vile sex thoughts keep popping up and the lady would be shocked and horrified to recognize them as her own, she is likely to get the idea, sooner or later, that they are coming from outside. That's it! A lot of men are after her, all of them up to no good. They are plotting and planning to submit her to all sorts of sexual outrages. Maybe they are going to perpetrate the outrages themselves, or perhaps they plan to capture her and sell her off to Arabian slave traders for shipment to some harem.

In mild cases of this sort the unfortunate female may have no more than misty fears of being accosted by some sinful male. If the feeling is a little more intense, she may start looking under the bed at night for a lustful burglar who may be hiding there. If the projection gets serious, she may tell people that lecherous men are pursuing her. She may even scream out accusations at some chance man on the street who never saw her before and never wants to see her again. If the delusions persist, the woman may ultimately have to be institutionalized.

There is an old folk saying that covers projection pretty well: "Don't judge other people by yourself." The man who always accuses others of trying to cheat him often has a desire himself to cheat and swindle but cannot admit it. He is suspicious that there is dishonesty around, and since he cannot admit that *he* has a tendency to be dishonest, he will insist that other people are dishonest. And so it goes through a long list. Someone who has a tendency to be jumpy may snap at someone else, "You make me nervous!" thus projecting the blame for his own anxiety.

Just to keep things in balance, I might say that noble as well as evil feelings can be projected. There is the kind, honest simpleton who thinks that everybody else is kind and honest too. Of course, he may get over it after being sold some fraudulent stock that is sure to triple in price in just a few weeks. Gullible Mr. Simpleton never stops to think that if the stock were really that wonderful, the promoters would keep it for themselves.

How does projection apply to alcoholism? In several ways. A common performance is for the drunk to project the blame for his condition onto another person or onto outside circumstances in general. What the guzzler wants is a drink; so he takes it and then shunts the blame elsewhere.

Of course, a drinker may really be so harassed by persons or circumstances that he is "driven to drink"; but that is less common than some of the alibi-manufacturing drinkers care to admit. The more common pattern is to want the drink first, then to project the blame.

Projection also operates in many of the resentments that we hear so much about in A.A. An active alcoholic feels upset and violent about one thing or another. He does not want to accept these feelings as his own; so he pushes them outside and attributes them to someone else. Most likely that is why a lot of drinkers in delirium tremens think that someone is out to kill them. They themselves would like to kill someone, perhaps themselves, and their own violent feelings are projected outside.

Three Stages to Despair: I-F-D

Now we come to a sequence of attitudes. I have borrowed it from the semanticist Wendell Johnson's book *People in Quandaries* (New York: Harper & Brothers, 1946). The book will repay reading by alcoholics or by anyone else. It was one of the many that I read in my own slow recovery from active alcoholism. Right now I shall give only a little bit of it, the I-F-D sequence. Johnson calls it the "IFD disease," from Idealism, to Frustration, to Demoralization. I like to call it Idealism, Frustration, Despair. Despair and demoralization are similar in many respects; my own terminology is just a little briefer.

The first stage is that someone has an idea or an ideal that he hopes to realize. He fails, however, to realize it. Perhaps the ideal is too vague. Perhaps it is unrealistic or impossible. At any rate, there is a shining vision or great aspiration, which can be almost anything. Thus we have teen-agers who want to get rich quick as performers—perhaps by banging on a banjo and singing foolish songs. But only a few have talent enough to catch on; all the rest catch it in the neck and never make the grade.

We have the fat girl who is teaching in a little country school—though she longs to be an airline hostess. We have county courthouse politicians who dream of becoming President of the United States. Many other aspirations and ideals that are not as extreme are nevertheless just as impossible; perhaps it is only a frustrated ambition to be president of the local Parent-Teachers Association.

Anyway, the ideal, aspiration, or ambition is not satisfied. The person may struggle and strive, but is frustrated and gets nowhere. He is stopped dead in his tracks. He wants something keenly but can't get it. As a result he may become anxious and unhappy. Time passes; things do not become better but instead seem to become worse as the shining vision continually dances on the horizon like a mirage. So the sufferer begins to curse and condemn himself as a failure.

If the initial drive and energy pushing toward the great ideal have been lost, the sense of failure gradually lapses into lethargy, hopelessness, and boredom. Or if some energy remains, it may all be invested in feelings of wild, raging, hopeless despair—which is the last stage of this very unfortunate sequence.

I don't need to go into the horrors of despair, since most of us have felt it at one time or another. In many, many cases, the I-F-D sequence can be quite alcoholic. First the grandiose dreams while filled with soothing drams, next the frustration and the attempt to drink away anxiety that is beginning to verge on panic, and last the complete and utter demoralization and despair of the well-advanced alcoholic.

The remedy is easy for me to write about, but hard for you to apply. Put the cork in the bottle; then cultivate a different outlook on life and its possibilities. If you don't find any good ideas in this book, look elsewhere. But *do something!*

Psychotherapy and Alcoholism

I have mentioned that I had to go in for several forms of psychotherapy to arrest my alcoholism. Back in 1945 when I was gradually building up into alcoholism, I had some Jungian psychotherapy that helped to some extent in easing my feelings of resentment, anxiety, guilt, and all the rest, although it had no effect in sobering me up. I continued with the alcohol as a means of easing the emotional torments which that particular brand of psychotherapy did not relieve.

Meanwhile my capacity for liquor kept building up. I was at the peak of my glory in 1948. I remember being at a drinking party in that year. When it was all over, someone said to someone else, who later reported it back to me, "Who was that peculiar-looking guy at the party? He drank and drank all evening but never got more than a little bit drunk!" This comment flattered me immensely. I had deep inferiority feelings at the time—but at least I could pour the stuff down and hold it down and stagger about.

But after hitting my peak of alcoholic glory, I began to lose my capacity. Less and less liquor got me more and more demoralized. That is one reason why I contacted A.A. in 1949. It did not stop me from drinking but it slowed me down a bit. Meanwhile I read heavily and examined all sorts of doctrines in an attempt to solve my problems and difficulties. About 1950, I went in heavily for General Semantics; it helped somewhat, but I won't bother you with that now.

Then about 1952–54 (before I finally stopped drinking for good, in 1956), I got a good deal of Gestalt therapy from Dr. Perls and his associates. It was very helpful, and I have incorporated some of it in this book.

Some definitions may be in order. Psychotherapy is an effort by a psychotherapist to modify a patient's unsuitable and abnormal thoughts, feelings, and patterns of behavior, usually by talking with the patient. In A.A. there is informal psychotherapy of a sort—done in an attempt to get some drunk to stop drinking and to modify his thoughts, feelings, and behavior. But generally the term psychotherapy is used for the efforts of someone trained and qualified to deal with unsuitable emotions and behavior.

Psychiatry is psychotherapy done by a physician with an M.D. degree. Usually the M.D. has had special training as a psychiatrist. The most common procedure is for the physician to talk with the patient in an effort to get him to change his emotional and behavioral patterns. Since most alcoholics and others with emotional disturbances became that way over a considerable period of time, a good many sessions are usually needed before the patient is able to absorb new patterns of thinking, feeling, and reacting.

Consulting a psychiatrist does not necessarily mean that a person is "crazy" or insane. Most persons in that extreme condition must be institutionalized. The term "insanity" is a legal concept, applying to cases of mental disturbance such that the person has no clear idea of right or wrong and is not responsible for his actions. Medical men usually let lawyers talk about insanity. They themselves prefer to use the term "psychosis" or "psychotic."

Most of the human race, including the alcoholic minority, are not psychotic but are more or less neurotic. That means that they are not living completely in a private world of their own, out of touch with accepted notions of reality; instead they are looking at life through lenses that appreciably distort things. They are subect to excessive emotional reactions; they do not operate at maximum efficiency; and they have more painful and disturbing feelings than pleasant ones. And so on through a long list of emotional and rational twists, distortions, and misdirections.

Freud contended that in every neurosis there are one or more conflicts; that is, the neurotic tends to think or feel or do one thing or another but also tends to think or feel or do pretty much the opposite. Most alcoholics know what that is like; we have had dreadful struggles between an impulse to drink and an opposite feeling that we ought not to drink, at least not at that particular moment. The person is the field of a one-man civil war, with opposing forces grappling and contending within him so that he is in a constant process of being torn apart by conflicting emotions.

Under such conditions a person may talk with friends, or seek spiritual help, or perhaps go to a psychiatrist or other psychotherapist. Perplexities of this sort provoke a great deal of public humor. It may be funny to outsiders, but to the mixed-up sufferers it is far from funny.

In magazine and newspaper cartoons the psychiatrist almost always wears a small beard and puts the patient on a couch where all sorts of amusing remarks are gotten off by the distraught "nut." That sort of thing is really psychoanalysis; the patient is supposed to lie on a couch and retail everything that he happens to experience in the way of thoughts or emotions. Such a performance is known as "free association." Usually the remarks, I am told, are not particularly witty or amusing. The patient just goes on and on rambling verbally. A session commonly lasts about an hour.

The couch procedure with the psychoanalyst out of sight of the patient was developed by Sigmund Freud, the founder of psychoanalysis. If the patient talks long enough, particularly about events of the past, the analyst may finally discern some common thread running through the wandering remarks. At this point the analyst may intervene with an interpretation of the meaning of the remarks. It is also supposed to be of importance to observe what the patient does *not* talk about. There may be a painful feeling attached to some topic that the patient wants to avoid. The analyst may ask a question or two and try to prod the patient into talking about something that he would rather not talk about.

Briefly, the idea developed by Freud was that emotional disturbances ultimately stem from emotional shocks in early life. If the original painful memory can be recovered and faced, then the results are supposed to be curative of emotional disturbances going on at the present time.

Now, in classical Freudian psychoanalysis, the things bothering the patient are supposed to be mainly sexual. This point of view has caused a great deal of controversy. Away back before World War I, two of Freud's students, Carl Jung and Alfred Adler, decided that Freud was overstressing the sexual basis of neurotic and other emotional disturbances. So each of them branched off and set up a school of his own. Later on, several other psychoanalysts branched off from the Freudian school. There are now perhaps a dozen kinds of psychoanalysis, each with a somewhat different theoretical basis.

After reading and pondering over dozens of books on psychotherapy and psychoanalysis, and after being subjected to some of the Gestalt form of psychoanalysis, I have arrived at some conclusions that may have a certain practical value.

First of all, psychoanalysis seems to me to be a rather inefficient way of going at things. The psychoanalyst ordinarily tends to be rather passive and may make a comment only now and then. Some persons may work out and resolve their troubles merely by talking about them; but I doubt if it is generally true. A good many people have emotional troubles that are so obvious that almost any intelligent person listening to them will get *some* idea of what is bothering them. If so, some comments from the listener may be in order. This was one advantage of the Gestalt approach that I was subjected to; it was a two-way performance and the therapist gave me a verbal prod when he thought that I needed one.

Dr. Perls with his Gestaltism did not go in for the psychoanalytical approach too strongly. He made what seems to me to be a worthwhile change in the procedures; namely, going after the obvious troubles first, getting in contact with the things that were right on the surface, instead of probing into the remote past for the very first emotional disturbance of a series.

By working with my emotional troubles of current interest, right then and there, the more deeply buried stuff had a certain tendency to rise to the surface and become more readily accessible. It is all of ten years since I had any Gestalt therapy, and I may be misinterpreting in retrospect, but that is my general impression of what happened to me. When a good many superficial emotional troubles were relieved, then some deeper ones came to the surface—like big boulders being thrown out of the ground by the frost—so that *they* could be dealt with in turn. Some of them I was able to deal with myself, by diligently digging into the psychological books, long after formal psychotherapy had ceased.

It appears to me that Freudian and other forms of psychoanalysis have turned into something that is more fashionable than effective. Psychoanalysis seems to have developed into a kind of cult or set of cults, surrogate religions as it were, claiming to offer a sort of salvation in this life—limited to true believers only! I am also dubious of the claims of Freud, Jung, Adler, and all the rest as to the general causes of all neurotic disturbances. My guess is that the alleged causes of emotional disturbances are very true in a limited number of cases—but that they are not of necessity *generally* true.

Some day, if the present book proves to be useful, I may go back and thoroughly examine the theories of Freud, Jung, Adler, and others from the standpoint of alcoholism. But now I shall press on to some fairly simple and fairly effective procedures that can be applied by almost anyone whose brain has not been totally destroyed by strong waters.

Where Do We Go From Here?

I have touched so lightly on a few schools of psychotherapy that I feel almost apologetic—almost but not quite. Although the various schools of psychotherapy and psychoanalysis have something to offer to the tormented alcoholic, I consider that their major lack is in not being specifically oriented toward alcoholism. So I shall be an empiricist of the wildest description and drag in stuff from all over the map in hopes that some of it will apply helpfully to at least some alcoholics. For years I have been whacking around at A.A. meetings, giving off this and that idea to see how it works. As a result I have worked up an assortment of approaches and methods that seem to be definitely helpful in many cases.

For one thing, in dealing with their own alcoholism and that of others, many alcoholics expect too much too soon. Alcoholism is a kind of neurosis or at least involves a lot of neurotic reactions sooner or later. If you were not neurotic when you began to drink, you will be by the time you feel that you ought to quit or must quit.

One aspect of neurosis is that the person is in a lot of emotional tangles and difficulties, but he wants to get over them in a flash, by applying some magic formula or set of magic formulas. In my opinion, that is one weakness of the A.A. twelve steps. Admittedly they have proven useful to thousands of persons; but, alas, they have not worked for thousands of others. Those who are helped stay around in A.A. and usually they cheer loudly for the twelve steps, or if they have not been particularly helped by the steps, at least they feel compelled to give them lip service.

Thousands of others are *not* particularly helped by the steps, or anything else that they encounter in A.A. Some of them are bound to fail; they want a magic cure and none is available. Once in a while we hear of a "miracle"; someone came into A.A., stopped drinking immediately, and never drank again. Such cases are exceptional. One form taken by the desire for a quick arrest of alcoholism is the hope of hearing someone utter some magic words that will suddenly, totally, and completely destroy all desire for alcohol. Again, such things do happen, but they are rather rare and certainly not to be counted upon. That was one of my troubles. For several years I bounced onto the bottle, and then when trouble ensued I bounced back to A.A. I always had the rather neurotic hope of some evening hearing a great and brilliant fellow pour out golden words that would wash away my craving for drink. It never happened. Instead, when all my capacity was gone, I had to stop by myself, and suffer by myself, and finally continue along the path of sobriety by applying a gamut of approaches that I had gathered up from all sorts of sources.

Finally I encountered something called R-E-P—Rational Emotive Psychotherapy. I prefer to shorten it a bit to Rational Emotive Therapy and call it R-E-T. This was two years after I stopped drinking, but by applying R-E-T to other persons (mainly those who did not benefit to a maximum extent from standard A.A.) it was possible to get some of them to turn sober and actually to like it rather well.

First Steps in Self-Psychotherapy

Although many neurotic alcoholics are sorely in need of psychotherapy, only a minority ever get any. Much of the psychotherapy available can be described as rather tangential; that is, it helps to some extent with some emotional disturbances but it frequently does not hit too directly on the *main* things that are troubling the alcoholic. Also, most forms of psychotherapy are rather expensive, particularly psychoanalysis. At a cost of, say, twenty-five dollars an hour, a person can readily run up a big bill in even a relatively few sessions of ordinary face-to-face psychotherapy. Furthermore, in many places few practitioners are available, and those few may be rushed to death trying to handle really rough cases of psychosis and extreme neurotic reactions; they don't have the time to give to ordinary alcoholics.

The situation, though bad, is not hopeless. It is possible to do quite a bit by oneself and for oneself if one recognizes that something is wrong and needs to be corrected. Very well; where do we start? I recommend reading and rereading a good, sensible, down-to-earth book entitled *How to Live With a Neurotic*, by Dr. Albert Ellis (New York: Crown Publishers, Inc.) It is one of the best things ever written in the field of self-help in psychotherapy. I met Dr. Ellis only once, but by constant reading of this book and one or two of his other books, I was able to improve my emotional state considerably. And I was also able to help other alcoholics.

In theory, the book was written as a sort of home manual or perhaps a general manual for people who must live or work with others who have neurotic disturbances. However, there is no reason why we cannot apply the book to ourselves! That is what I did, and anyone who wants to can do likewise.

When the book was first published in 1957, Dr. Ellis was still developing his methods of R-E-T. Hence it is not a finished work; nevertheless, it contains elements of great value. Probably anyone of normal intelligence who will read it and then reread it again and again will gain something useful each time. I don't say that everyone will; but the book is at least worth a thorough trial. Material garnered from R-E-T is scattered throughout the present book; so if you get anything out of it, it will probably pay you to go on to the Ellis book.

The basis of R-E-T is the theory that neurotic reactions can start in all kinds of ways, but that they are kept going by people talking to themselves and continually reinjecting or reinoculating themselves with negativistic and disturbing ideas that serve to continue the neuroses. In later sections, I'll throw in hunks and chunks of R-E-T as interpreted by myself. I think that they are at least moderately good; and if you want something better, you can go to the works of Dr. Ellis as the original fount of this form of methodology and wisdom.

Some of the books of Dr. Ellis deal extensively with various sex questions. Some persons think that his attitudes on sex are a little extreme; however, persons who are upset by his outspoken attitude can skip that part of the Ellis writings if they wish.

What Will the Neighbors Say?

One gigantic cause of emotional disturbance delineated by Dr. Ellis is the idea that nearly everybody ought to love you or like you, or at least not dislike you. In vain attempts to win universal approval, or at least to avoid disapproval, countless people tear themselves to bits every day in the year.

This situation is certainly common here in America. It crops out in all kinds of ways. I don't know how this "I must please everyone" attitude got started, but there are indications that it may be connected with theories about child-rearing that have recently been in vogue.

In the bad old days small children who misbehaved oftentimes received wallopings or other drastic punishment. Then a swing began toward a "permissive" attitude, which in its turn quite possibly went too far. Anyway, a good many children were brought up with an absolute minimum of corporal discipline. Instead, dear, loving Mother said, in substance, "That is naughty and you must not do it. If you do things like that, Mother won't love you any more. And other people won't *like* you." So, possibly as a result, millions of Americans grew up to adult years with a feeling that social disapproval, however senseless and baseless, was one of the most awful things in life, to be anxiously avoided at all costs.

In *Reason and Emotion in Psychotherapy* (New York: Lyle Stuart, 1962), Dr. Ellis calls this kind of outlook on life Irrational Idea No. 1: "The idea that it is a dire necessity for an adult human being to be loved or approved by virtually every significant other person in his community." The newspapers were once filled with clamor about this or that criminal who was "public enemy number one." We might call this mad love of applause and approval "internal enemy number one." It is a "monkey on the back" of millions of people who spend their days in fear that someone will not like them and may do something drastic to them.

To paraphrase a few useful thoughts from Dr. Ellis, a mad yearning for the approbation of others is bound to be a hopelessly losing game. Even if the vast majority of your associates approved of you most highly, there would always be a few who did not. And most likely you would take the approval of the majority for granted and tear out your heart and soul, your liver and your lights, in frantic and hopeless attempts to win over the minority who did not like you. And you might get to fussing and fuming about whether the majority approved of you still. That can lead to pretty severe anxiety. It is not exactly the kind of anxiety mentioned in the R-A-G concept, although it borders on it.

Then again, no one can be affable and noble all of the time. And if you have an occasional bad day when you feel out of sorts and grumpy, you will get to feeling much worse if you let yourself think that everybody is bound to hate and despise you for not gurgling with sweetness and light.

Even if it were possible, hypothetically, to impress favorably everyone with whom you come in contact, you would need to put so much time and energy into the pursuit of approval that you would have little left for other activities. And in trying constantly to obtain approval you are apt to become subservient or ingratiating—qualities that are bound to irritate a certain number of people, so that your efforts would automatically become self-defeating.

I do not mean to suggest that you can or should be so self-centered as to rub a lot of people the wrong way. It is certainly worthwhile to be pleasant and agreeable with family, friends, and associates, short of crawling in the dust and currying favor with them. And if frictions develop nevertheless, the sensible thing to do is to try to correct the frictions if at all possible.

Perhaps it all boils down to the question "What do I want to do in life?" rather than "What do other people want me to do?" We can't do all things that we would like to do, but we certainly can do some of them. Hence, adopting a judicious compromise between what we want and what other people want may, after all, be the best course. But there is not much sense in trying to win the approval of others when their disapproval means little or nothing. If there is a clear and present danger that they will hit you a whack, or burn your house down, or get you fired from your job, then you may need to placate and appease them. But such extreme situations are rare. Much more common is to have a general haunting feeling—pervasive and convincing because you never stop to analyze it—that you must do such and such because if you do not, you will be criticized. The question to ask yourself might well run as follows: "If I do such and such then so-and-so will disapprove of it. But what if they do disapprove of it, provided I am not harming someone overtly? Just what punishment or revenge are they going to inflict on me?"

Then, if your course of action is not factually harmful, you can go ahead and follow it knowing that whatever you did, someone would be upset about it if he happened to know about it. So if you try to please everyone you may end by displeasing everyone, including yourself—and that is the worst fate of all.

I had a great-grandmother who was known as a fierce old lady. She is alleged to have said, "Suit yourself, for God knows you can't suit anybody else." I finally had to adopt this ancestral motto as a personal slogan. I have handed it on to other A.A. members. Some of them liked it. I now hand it on to any A.A. member (or anyone else) who reads this book. As long as you are off the alcohol and not doped up in any other way, you are in good A.A. standing no matter what anyone thinks about you.

Hitting Bottom

One alcoholic performance often spoken of in A.A. is the process of "hitting bottom." This means that alcohol has gotten a person into so many kinds of trouble so many times that he has nothing left to do except to stop drinking or to die off—or perhaps spend the rest of his life in a penal institution for having committed some crime while drunk, or else in a mental institution. Both death and deprivation of liberty are unpleasant; so when either point seems to be approaching, some alcoholics will stop drinking.

At A.A. meetings one frequently hears graphic descriptions by speakers on when and how they hit bottom. Oftentimes it is a process involving multiple arrests for intoxication, multiple jail sentences perhaps, multiple commitments to mental institutions, multiple marriages, and multiple divorces, as well as the multiple losses of successive jobs. Alcoholics who must undergo all kinds of dreadful punishments before they are ready to quit in A.A. are called "low-bottom drunks."

Fortunately not all alcoholics are that bad. A good many realize when their drinking is taking an undesirable turn and are able to stop before anything too drastic happens to them. Such cases are called "high-bottom drunks." Formerly they were relatively uncommon; most A.A. members were in the low-bottom category. But of late years, more people stop drinking before reaching any terminal stage of total disaster. This is a hopeful development.

My guess as to what keeps people from stopping in the earlier stages is that nearly all of them hate to recognize that the alcohol which once seemed to be such a friend is slowly developing into a subtle, inexorable enemy. They are constantly seeking to recover the warm and pleasant alcoholic magic of an earlier day; but the magic is irregularly fading out of the picture. The process is oftentimes a slow one, and for limited periods a developing alcoholic can often continue to drink without too much trouble. But in many such cases, if not all, the progression goes on and on and terminates in disaster.

In other cases, people lose the ability to enjoy alcohol but are caught up in a compulsion and feel that they *must* go on drinking. For these there is nothing to be done but to get them off the alcohol for a time until the compulsion lessens or disappears.

It might help greatly if A.A. were to adopt a policy of welcoming all persons who had *any degree* of trouble with alcohol. Instead full-fledged A.A. members too often buttonhole the newcomer and question him to find out definitely whether he thinks he is or is not an alcoholic. I have even heard of persons being chased away from A.A. because the members, usually of the low-bottom variety, thought the newcomer not sufficiently qualified.

My influence in A.A. councils is small. But I am going to make a definite and concrete suggestion, in fact a recommendation. If the powers who guide the destinies of A.A. wished to expand the scope, the helpfulness, and the usefulness of A.A., they could do it very simply.

They could do it by making it a definite policy to encourage the attendance, at closed as well as at open meetings, of all who thought they might be *possible* or *potential* alcoholics. On a somewhat tenuous and theoretical basis, this may already be so. On an actual working basis, it generally is not so. Most members at closed meetings seem to insist on a sort of verbal formula from anyone who makes an appearance more than once or twice. Sooner or later the newcomer is supposed to chirp out something to the effect, "I am Juggy Johnson, and I'm an alcoholic" or "I am Beulah Bottle, and I'm an alcoholic."

On this rather narrow and rigid basis, there is little or no room for those persons who have a creeping feeling that they are or may be gradually getting there but have not yet arrived. If the protocol-minded A.A. element insist on some statement of status or qualifications, I see no objection to somebody stating "I am Nick the Nipper, and I am possibly an alcoholic" or perhaps "I am Tillie the Tippler, and I sometimes drink too much." If such dubious or borderline cases can be saved before they fall over the edge into the alcoholic abyss, all to the good!

I am going to be tiresome again by putting in another plug for A.A. Tradition No. 3: "The only requirement for A.A. membership is a desire to stop drinking." Either that means what it says or else it does not. If it does mean what it says, then I intend to raise a howl from time to time to try to make it stick. But if it does not mean what it says, then it should be dropped, and a new and different tradition interpolated in its place. The tradition says nothing at all about how strong the desire to stop drinking must be; it says nothing at all about how long the desire must last. On that basis even a transitory desire to stop drinking is a full qualification for A.A. membership.

"The Tyranny of the Should"

One of the sharpest and brightest former followers of Freud was Karen Horney (pronounced horn-eye). Dr. Horney diverged somewhat from the theories of Freud after she came to America and wrote several books developing psychotherapy on a different basis. They are worth reading. I heard Dr. Horney speak a few times and found her rather thick German accent hard to follow, but her books are beautifully written. Her last and best book, in my opinion, is *Neurosis and Human Growth* (New York: W. W. Norton & Co., 1950). I recommend it highly to anyone interested in searching for the sources of his emotional troubles. Chapter three is entitled "The Tyranny of the Should." I shall not give any of it verbatim, but shall adapt some of the ideas for the benefit of those with alcoholic or other neuroses.

In brief, many people are obsessed with the false and foolish notion that they should be great wonders, and tremendously capable, competent, and brilliant in almost all fields of human effort. Dr. Albert Ellis expresses this conviction as Irrational Idea No. 2 of his listing: "The idea that one should be thoroughly competent, adequate, and achieving in all possible respects if one is to consider oneself worthwhile."

And that is quite a large order. But millions suffer from this foolish obsession, in our current state of civilization. Just how it comes about, I don't know; but most likely it is the result of early training by parents and teachers, later reinforced by magazines, newspapers, radio, television, and other media. They beat, beat, beat at us with the idea that we *should* do this, we *should* do that, we *should* do the other. The shoulds that are thrown at us every day in the year are without any limit, in contrast to our limited capacity to measure up to all these shoulds. It is like several thousand people all wanting to pile their belongings on some pack animal and force the beast to carry a prodigious load far beyond any reasonable capacity. It makes no sense at all.

Nevertheless, many people are so browbeaten in their youth into thinking that they *must* carry any burden thrust upon them that they really take this nonsense seriously. They feel that they should measure up to and handle any should that is thrust upon them. To do less would be to admit failure and deep unworthiness. So they go through life trying to measure up to all sorts of preposterous and impossible demands. They may resist such demands in childhood; but that attitude is finally beaten out of them, perhaps not with a stick, but with a bombardment of words from parents, teachers, and others.

To make this whole thing tangible, I'll give two hypothetical cases—one a man, the other a woman. I shall lay it on thick, but perhaps not *too* thick.

The two people whose sad lives I shall touch upon are Mr. I. M. Zunk and his wife. These imaginary characters have far more nobility of spirit than ordinary sense in their makeup. They are willing to accept any sort of should that is thrown in their direction.

Mr. Zunk is imbued with should ideas. He should support his wife and three children according to the highest standards laid down in the advertisements. He should live in a good house in a good neighborhood. He should rake in money by the barrel to pay for it all. He should get a new car every year, and maybe provide an extra car for Mrs. Zunk. Mr. Zunk should never be tired. No matter what happens, he should be filled with cheery optimism. He should get a promotion or at least a raise every year or so. He should be a model parent and should see that his children get the best possible education. He should be an active church member. He should belong to several clubs to uphold his social status. He should give generously to every charity that barks in his direction; yet, on the other hand, he should save his money and he should carry insurance against all contingencies.

He should be active in politics and civic affairs. He should watch his figure and guard against overweight and heart attacks. Mr. Zunk really has a load to carry. But wait! I'm not finished yet. I can't let Mr. Zunk off *too* easily.

In addition to his duties as a perfect pillar of the community, Mr. Zunk should have another side to his nature; at least he often thinks he should. If he doesn't think so, some self-styled he-man will get hold of dopey old Zunk and convince him otherwise. What I mean is that Mr. Zunk should measure up to all the standards set by the professional red-blooded male element that he associates with. He should laugh at off-color jokes and he should tell some himself—but of course the jokes should not be *too* smutty. At business luncheons he should join in with the boys and should drink enough martinis so that no one else will feel uncomfortable. At conventions he should get drunk to just the proper degree and he should cut up in other respects if someone else thinks that he should. When he is slopped, he should be funny (not messy) and he should always have enough control to take care of anyone else who is slopped worse than he is. In a word, his alcoholic ideal should be to drink like a gentleman, but at the same time he should uphold virile hard-drinking standards.

He should keep a big cabinet of liquor at home and he should push drinks at anyone who drops in. He should have a good assortment of booze on hand, else his social standing will suffer. He should have cocktails before dinner—the magazine ads say that he should, and all his associates agree. They too are filled with the same set of shoulds, and they should hold onto them; otherwise the American Way of Life (whatever that is) will come to a grinding halt—and depression, or worse, will stalk the land.

Now we'll go on to Mrs. Zunk. This poor woman thinks that she should be an absolutely model mother and housewife. Her home should always be spic-and-span, no matter how hard the struggle and no matter how thoroughly her family mess it up for her.

Mrs. Zunk reads and believes all the stuff in the women's

magazines. So she thinks that she should spend hours and hours every week cooking up concoctions that not only look good but taste good—absolute masterpieces. She should buy all sorts of vitamin pills and cram them into her family and herself. She should follow every flicker of fashion and wear all kinds of smart clothes. On the other hand, she should operate on a tight budget so as to save money for all the other shoulds that keep her harassed. She should be active in church work and cultural activities. She should drag her husband to Parent-Teacher Association (P.T.A.) meetings even when all the shoulds that *he* is carrying make him a trifle dopey, weary, and cranky. She should work fourteen hours a day keeping up with all her shoulds; yet when Mr. Zunk comes home after the proverbial hard day at the office, she should be full of sweetness and light, as chipper as a squirrel. Mrs. Zunk has dozens of other shoulds; but I am weary of recounting them, and no doubt the reader is weary of hearing about them. Anyway, in order to carry all her burdens while Mr. Zunk is away from home, Mrs. Zunk *may* start taking nips out of a bottle.

Mr. and Mrs. Zunk are that way because they foolishly let themselves be indoctrinated with too many false shoulds. Nothing will really help the Zunks in any basic way unless they can somehow throw overboard enough shoulds to make their lives at least halfway tolerable.

If the Zunks get to feeling too overburdened and tense, they may seek psychiatry for their troubles. They may get a sensible psychiatrist who will tell them that they are trying to be too much and to do too much, and that they could well ease off a bit. Maybe they would follow such advice, maybe not. Quite likely they would develop tremendous guilt feelings about dropping any of their shoulds, so that the psychiatrist would have another problem to deal with in addition to the original one. Or they may get a rather uninspired psychiatrist who will merely make some vague general comments on their sad case and then prescribe tranquilizers. Medication with tranquilizers certainly has its place at times. But tranquilizers are not going to effect anything remotely resembling a cure in people whose pattern of living is fundamentally faulty.

And now I'll just have to leave the Zunks with their sufferings. But if the reader can understand that it is not possible to be an absolute whiz-bang and to play Superman and Wonder Woman in each and every department of human life, the poor Zunks will not have suffered in vain. Their fate will serve as a warning to others not to try to be too great, too noble, and too wonderful!

Life Is Not Fair!

Life is not fair! No, it certainly is not. All of us were born into it without asking for it. Nevertheless, most of us start out in youth with high and vaulting hopes, ambitions, and aspirations. But for many of us, things soon go wrong and there is an awful mess! Maybe the mess is financial, or occupational, or sexual; but in any event we find ourselves in a mess. This book is for people for whom the mess, or at least an important part of it, happens to be alcoholic.

Possibly the chief trouble is that few of us were taught by our parents and our teachers to deal with human existence as it actually is. Instead we were taught to deal with it on the basis of what someone or other thinks it should be—but isn't. One way or another we picked up a lot of glamorous and goofy notions about things as they ought to be—but aren't! Quite often we were pumped full of high ideals of the sort that could work only under ideal conditions—which never occurred. Among other illusions we were taught to believe that there is some kind of justice in life—when most of the experience of the human race tends to point to the contrary.

We sought for "fairness" and "justice" and we found little. Instead other people seemed always to be playing mean tricks on us, and fate seemed to deal out an interminable series of harsh blows. We got into situations that made grim jokes of the copybook maxims about ambitions and ideals. To dull our hopelessness, despair, remorse, anxiety, and other sad and tortured emotions we turned to alcohol—which in turn failed us.

It's a grim picture that I paint. Since I am a bit of a fiend (according to some A.A. members who don't agree with me), I get a fiendish delight in making things out to be pretty awful. However, they are not hopeless; rather, life can be appreciably better, at least for most people, after a certain shift or change in attitude.

Long ago I picked up a saying: "Never expect too much of any human being or any human institution. In that way you will never be disappointed." I think that's a good principle to keep in mind. A lot of situations are not quite what we would like them to be. But by pressing an emotional claim or demand that they *should* be better and different, we make them a great deal worse than they need to be.

People are engaged in doing all sorts of things that they think they are doing for their own benefit. Actually, a good many of them are deluded in their efforts; but they keep up the efforts just the same. Or perhaps they think that they are helping themselves by avoiding effort. Anyway, they are up to something or other. Normal individuals are behaving more or less normally, neurotics are behaving neurotically, and the minority who are psychotics are behaving psychotically. But by and large, they are all trying to look out for themselves, whether they admit it or not. A few may be trying to act altruistically; but even these few will shelve the altruism if it begins to clash with their own interests.

In all this crowd who are acting and interacting this way and that way, there is never going to be much help for those who think that they are somehow entitled to be pleased, suited, and gratified on the basis of some abstract ideal of justice or fairness. Sooner or later the rest of the milling mass of humanity are going to stamp on their toes and hurt them severely.

It is not fair. It is not just. But it *is!*

So, to avoid undue suffering in life, it is well to be on guard. One need not be eternally suspicious. One need not lead a greatly restricted life to avoid trouble. But it is well to maintain an awareness that other people can very possibly take advantage of us, and to take reasonable and sensible measures to prevent them from doing us any extreme harm. People are looking out for themselves. And usually they are looking out for themselves more pointedly when they offer us something—when they paint a beautiful word picture of what great benefits will be ours if only we will do something that they want us to do. Sometimes they will treat us fairly; but other times they will not.

Human relationships shift and change. Today's friend may be tomorrow's foe. There is no justice or fairness to it; the situation simply is. And going back to the three possible points given elsewhere in this book, it is realistic to treat oneself reasonably well and to treat others reasonably well. The latter policy can be followed to good advantage even when others seriously offend or injure us— perhaps!

There is said to be a saying in China that it is not good to break an enemy's rice bowl—meaning that extreme retaliation against real or supposed injustice and unfairness is not prudent. There are a lot of other sayings in folklore about injustice and how to react to it. A maxim of Spanish origin is so deliciously and wisely cynical that I treasure it dearly: "Always treat a friend as if he may some day be an enemy, and always treat an enemy as if he may some day be a friend."

To return to an old theme: The booze won't help us too much even if in fact we have been hideously wronged. Maybe it will for a while; but in the end it ceases to be a balm to the tortured spirit. "Look not upon the wine when it is red, for in the end it biteth like a serpent and stingeth like an adder."

More on Those Terrible Resentments

In an earlier section I said that in A.A. it is customary to regard resentments as Just Simply Terrible—but that I don't have quite such an adverse opinion of them. A lot of alcoholics, however, do have resentments and in many cases the usual attempts to more or less talk them or preach them away simply don't work.

Once upon a time, when I had some emotional jimjams, I consulted a psychiatrist who was pretty much of a Freudian. In some ways his comments on my reactions were helpful, but in other ways they were not. He kept fishing around for guilt feelings—but they had been pretty well flushed out by the Gestalt therapy I had received several years previously.

Finally the psychiatrist asked me right out what it was that I felt guilty about. When I replied that I didn't feel particularly guilty about much of anything but that I felt resentful about a lot of things, he curled up like a caterpillar with astonishment. Apparently he was used to handling cases that were all eaten up with guilt, and case-hardened alcoholics with resentments were a novelty to him. At least that is how I look at it.

Well, to get a bit theoretical about it, I *may* have gotten rid of a load of guilt feelings by projecting them or externalizing them onto other people. Anyway, I felt much better with a goodly collection of resentments roosting on me externally than with a big load of guilt feelings gnawing away at me inside! I sometimes had a fantasy that the resentments were buzzards roosting on my shoulders, ready to fly off and bite people who had done me wrong.

Another way of dealing with resentments is to ease off as much as you can on blame and moral judgments directed against others as well as against oneself. About three-quarters of the time, when people pull something on you that you regard as unfair, morally reprehensible, and unjustified, they themselves regard their actions as totally and completely justified. They want something really badly, and nearly all the time they can satisfy their own consciences that their actions are quite proper.

I sometimes put it this way: If you were in a place that was full of rats, roaches, and rattlesnakes, it would not be surprising if some of these creatures were to bite you, or nibble on you, or sting you once in a while. But it would not be a moral issue. You couldn't be blamed for getting upset if a rat rushed out and bit you on the leg, but I don't think you would say that the rat had a bad moral character!

To a degree, and in a sense, the human world is something like the pit of vermin mentioned. A good many human beings are so neurotic and cracked that as far as their performances go, they are not much better than excited animals. The animals are not morally responsible for being what they are; similarly, a lot of human beings may not be *too* morally responsible for being what they happen to be. But it is up to you not to get bitten any more than you can help. And there is no need to go about biting yourself (retroflection) because things are in a bad way.

From a slightly different point of view, it would certainly be pleasant if everyone whom you encountered were to lay himself out to please, and suit, and satisfy *you* in all your wants, wishes, desires, and demands; but ordinary experience indicates that the world we live in is not organized that way. In any event, you certainly have no God-given right to *demand* that the rest of the people in the world accommodate themselves to you. If you can work it so that you are not the victim of too many real or supposed outrages, then you are doing very well indeed.

Still, some degree of resentment at real or supposed mistreatment is likely to remain with us. In that case, it may be well to cultivate a sort of grim humor about it all. If we can regard mistreatment as a piece of low stupidity on the part of the other fellow, as indeed it sometimes is, then the sting will not be so great. If we can regard "the exact nature of our wrongs" (in this case, the wrongs done to us) as being low exhibitions of boobery instead of cosmic outrages, then perhaps we can laugh about the situation a little bit, at least from time to time. I have no sure cure for resentments; but by one means or another it is possible to relax them quite noticeably.

I once knew an A.A. nicknamed Barbarous Barbara, who was the local lady resentment champion. Since I knew that I could not remove her resentments, I advised her to concentrate on them one hour a day and to do something else the rest of the time. But she moved away; and I never learned how my psychotherapy worked out.

Stay in the Driver's Seat—But Drive Safely!

Catch phrases and popular attitudes come and go in A.A. I remember back to where nearly every A.A. speaker had something to say about "alcoholic thought." I have not happened to hear that phrase in some time. Then there was a period when speakers kept talking about "getting A.A. by osmosis." That sounded important; but I don't think that most of them knew what they were talking about. Nor did I.

At the moment of writing, a lot of the speakers upbraid themselves by saying, "I was in the driver's seat" to explain some trouble they got into while drinking or perhaps when trying to stop drinking. Being in the driver's seat is regarded as being pretty wicked; most such speakers seem to feel that one should "let go and let God" instead.

The crux of the matter, it seems to me, is *how you act* in the driver's seat. If you get behind the wheel of a car and then roar down the road at ninety miles an hour, weaving back and forth with no regard for anyone else, trouble is likely to follow. But if you get over on the right side of the road, and stay alert, and drive at a reasonable speed, the chances of trouble are greatly diminished. Most people would say so.

If you get tired or sleepy, it will not make much sense to "let go and let God" guide your vehicle. If you just relax, and shut your eyes, and perhaps begin to pray—well, it may be very noble but it is not very intelligent. You are likely to fetch up in jail, on a hospital cot, or on a very cold slab in the morgue somewhere, despite all your piety.

There may be a grain of truth in regarding being "in the driver's seat" as deplorable, and an attitude of "let go and let

God" as being commendable. If being in the driver's seat means that you are attempting to impose your will on everybody and everything regardless of conditions and circumstances, then it is not a bright idea. You are attempting to impose that "tyranny of the should" on the rest of the world—and there will be trouble sooner or later.

As to the "let go and let God" end of things, I think that some ordinary sense will be helpful. It is often good to relax a bit and stop rushing about making a lot of demands. How God comes into the picture, I don't know. There are all kinds of beliefs and opinions about God. In any case, the "let go" end of things might be moderated a bit. If I let go so far that I never get up in the morning, and just lie in bed waiting for a flock of ravens to come in the window and feed me—like the prophet Elijah in the Bible story—then I can wait quite a long time. I might even become very, very hungry before the situation was resolved!

No doubt I am a monster to try to rob A.A. speakers of all their pat phrases. Maybe somebody should write a book giving me and all my ideas a good panning. I am waiting, waiting. Go to it, somebody! Even if I get roasted to a brown turn, it may be helpful to inject some new ideas into A.A.; there have been hardly any new ideas of value in the past twenty-five years. Someone "should" stir things up a little.

The Myerson Maneuver

I consider that the one outstanding source of trouble in helping people to stop drinking by A.A. methods is the prevalent idea that it must be done on some sort of "spiritual" basis. What this means in practice is that attempts are made to induce the drinker to accept the idea of God as some sort of "being" and possessing a "will" that can be, or may be, exerted to aid the alcoholic sufferer if only he will resort to the proper form of prayer. Step 11 of A.A. also mentions meditation, but speakers who mention meditation are few indeed.

The prayer approach is indeed good for persons with conventional views on religion; but it is not so good when applied to the atheists, agnostics, free-thinkers, skeptics, and just plain nonreligious and nonspiritual persons who also have alcoholic troubles.

I myself did not stop drinking completely and finally until I had been with A.A. for about seven years. About three-quarters of the trouble was with me, and I admit it. I did not want to stop drinking. The other one-quarter was that a lot of A.A.s insisted on tampering and fooling around with my views on religion and spirituality in a way that I could not and would not accept.

Finally I was able to stop drinking, but it was only after a couple of frightful fracases and verbal battles to the death in which I told a large number of people that I could not drink any more and that I was stopping—but that I declined to accept anything at all in the so-called spiritual part of the program that did not make sense to me as an individual.

About this time I read an interesting book, *Speaking of Man*, by Dr. Abraham Myerson (New York: Alfred A. Knopf, 1950). It is a bit on the skeptical side. I can recommend it to anyone who gets anything at all out of my book. I do not recommend it to anyone who must operate on the basis of believing a lot of things merely because someone tells him that he should believe them.

From Dr. Myerson I derived an approach that can be called "the Myerson maneuver." It is based on the idea that because someone must stop drinking, it does not mean that he must adopt someone else's spiritual or religious views. I quote Dr. Myerson:

> In my work I have never interfered in what I call the "fundamental values" of my patients. Whatever I may believe, negatively or positively, about religion, morality, and so on, has nothing to do with the value to my patient of these all-important matters. He may believe whatever he pleases about God and the angels; and whether he is an orthodox religionist or a complete atheist I can minister to him without destroying what is essential to his personal stability.

Having picked up this valuable approach, I have found that it usually works somewhat better than standard A.A. with its insistence on the twelve steps and a general foggy religiosity. A large mass of irrelevant side issues is avoided. After all, if some people do best by making a sort of quasi-religion out of their atheism or agnosticism, why confuse the fundamental alcoholic issue by trying to change their views on God and prayer?

Just by way of explanation, I'll say that my idea of God is that of an incomprehensible primordium that exists neither in space nor in time; yet everything that does exist in space and time arises out of this primordium. If someone else wants to anthropomorphize God as "the man upstairs," that is all right too. If getting in material about God and spirituality seems likely to help the individual alcoholic, then I am for it. If it only causes confusion, then it is best left alone. Any form of A.A. is good A.A. if it gets people off the liquor and helps them to stay off it.

This is not to say that the customary A.A. approach is never any good at all. That statement would be nonsense. But I am strongly persuaded that almost any means at all (short of unnecessary medication) that gets people to stop drinking alcohol can be approved of. This thought may rile persons with totalitarian tendencies, but I have seen too many drinkers in awful tangles because some conventional A.A. member insisted on getting in a lot of confusing spiritual material when the main issue was merely to get the drinkers to stop drinking. The objective is sobriety; how people get there is of small importance.

No Magic Formula Exists

A big stumbling block in dealing with alcoholism (and many other things in human life) is the idea that somewhere, away out behind the beyond, is a magic formula or set of magic formulas that will answer all questions, solve all problems, and resolve all difficulties. This is the attitude that led the alchemists to search for the philosopher's stone, the knights in the middle ages to search for the Holy Grail, and Ponce de León to search for the fountain of youth.

Dr. Ellis describes this sort of thinking under Irrational Idea No. 11: "The idea that there is invariably a right, precise, and perfect solution to human problems and that it is catastrophic if this perfect solution is not found."

As a result of this sort of attitude, millions of people accomplish very little in life. The things that they can actually do seem drab and gray. So they lose themselves in vagrant fantasies of somehow obtaining some miracle cure for all their troubles. Perhaps they actually go in search of the cure but get into blind trails that lead nowhere, and into lines of effort that yield but meager fruit.

This attitude makes trouble for people with alcoholic and other troubles. Some seek relief through psychoanalysis—chasing after some forgotten trauma or emotional shock in the past that got them unhinged in the first place. A third or a quarter of the time and money spent in face-to-face psychotherapy to deal with presently existing sources of emotional disturbance would usually produce the same or better results.

Other persons keep shifting around from one religion to another in hopes of someday finding the complete and absolute truth about human life and destiny. Still others go on travel binges, hoping that if they move from one part of the world to some other place, all their troubles will be left behind. But they always take themselves along, and wherever they go and whatever they do, they generally make inadequate efforts to change themselves and their reactions to life.

Alack and alas! In A.A. the search for a magic formula goes on all the time. People go to dozens of meetings in the course of a year and hear all kinds of speakers and all sorts of discussions. In many cases, they have an idea that if somehow they could only work all the twelve steps perfectly, all their woes would disappear. But they often fail to work on themselves. If they would persistently cultivate the things that move them away from the bottle and avoid the things that move them toward the bottle, acting according their own individual cases, there would be far fewer slips in A.A.

I know how it is. Once upon a time, I went to dozens and dozens of A.A. meetings hoping to hear some speaker who would end my craving for booze by the magic of his words. But it never happened. The craving always built up again after a time. So finally I had to do it *for myself* and *by myself*. I stayed out of circulation and remained at home until the worst of the craving had passed. Then I got back into circulation gradually, but I avoided places where liquor was available. After a long time my former habit of drinking was broken and I acquired a habit of not drinking. It was more a matter of habit formation than anything else. And as long as I don't get too tired, or hungry, or thirsty, or jittered up, I am likely to be all right.

The Theory of Partial Solutions

If we cannot be something absolutely wonderful and attain to great and magnificent things, what is left? The answer is that plenty is left. If you can't do something big, you might try doing something middle-sized. And if you can't do something middle-sized, you might try doing something small. And if you will make an effort to improve your situation, perhaps by as little as one or two per cent, there will be a cumulative effort and after a while things will be much better than before. All accomplishment requires some effort, and sometimes a great deal of effort is required to attain something quite limited and small.

For most of us the gap between unrealistic aspiration and actual performance is very wide, and usually gets wider as the years roll by. Then perhaps we get tanked up and for a few hours we live in a dreamland in which all these excessive aspirations are already accomplished. But it is only a fleeting dream. In the end an ounce of performance is worth a ton of dreams.

Perhaps the touchstone or criterion to use is an intrinsic and not an extrinsic one. Goals, objectives, and ambitions might well be based on what *we* are capable of and not on what somebody else is capable of. In writing this book I had a perfectly awful time. I kept flopping on the bed and imagining that the book was already written, and that it was the most stunning, deep, and remarkable product ever sparked off from a human brain. Beautiful dreams, but they got me nowhere. So finally, with many a groan and grunt, I applied the seat of my pants to a chair, my fingers to the typewriter keys, and my brain to the task at hand—and after a while the doggone book was finished. It is not the best book on alcoholism ever written; but after reading over some of the slop on the subject, I believe that it is not the worst.

It would be great if I could write such a splendid book on the curse of drink that all the alcoholics in the land would troop sobbing to my doorstep to drink in my words of wisdom. But it's not possible. So I just wrote a modest book; and maybe it will help some small percentage of alcoholics who read it. I'll just have to content myself with being a very minor prophet.

The McGoldrick and Tracy Approaches

Other approaches than A.A. exist that claim a measure of success with alcoholism. Edward J. McGoldrick, Jr., has written a useful book, *Management of the Mind* (New York: Houghton Mifflin Co., 1954), on the control of alcoholism. For some years he has been director of an institution called Bridge House, established by the city of New York to deal with alcoholism. Back in his drinking days, McGoldrick had some contact with A.A. but he objected to the A.A. doctrine that alcoholism is a disease. He considers alcoholism to be the result of erroneous thought processes and calls it a "personality disorder." I get the impression that he stresses the moral and religious aspects of alcoholism somewhat more strongly than is common in A.A.

McGoldrick has worked out seventeen principles of what he calls a "mental diet." These principles together with other methods of completely avoiding alcohol are given in a course of lectures lasting three weeks, followed by a minimum of three hours a week of instruction for the following year. That is the way things stood when McGoldrick wrote his book. He claims a recovery (complete abstinence) rate of 65 per cent for alcoholics whom he has handled.

I have not had any extensive contacts with anyone who has tried the McGoldrick approach, but a perusal of his book suggests that it would have considerable effectiveness. The main difficulty seems to be that the McGoldrick method is more or less localized around New York City, while A.A. has a nation-wide and even a world-wide distribution. This means that an alcoholic who has stopped drinking but who has begun to wobble a bit and who may crave support can nearly always get to an A.A. meeting or make an individual A.A. contact nearly anywhere in the United States. What would happen to a McGoldrick adherent under such conditions, I don't know. Anyway, McGoldrick has a Principle No. 4 in his mental diet to the effect that "I realize that I must not neglect my physical health." That is a good point, and I recommend it to some of the "spiritual" enthusiasts in A.A.

Another arrested alcoholic who has developed a system for dealing with alcoholism is Vincent Tracy, who operates an establishment at Tracy Farms, Coeymans Hollow, New York. Like Bill Wilson, Tracy was treated by Dr. Silkworth at Towns Hospital in New York City, and was induced to attend A.A. meetings. But he was badly upset by some of the horror tales that he heard, and like McGoldrick, he obected to calling alcoholism a disease. Tracy put in three weeks at Bridge House at one time. Later he set up the nonprofit Tracy Foundation.

Tracy's approach to alcoholism seems to be strongly religious. Tracy was born a Catholic but abandoned the church during his period of active drinking. Later, when his drinking was arrested, he returned to his former religious views. A description of Tracy's history and the development of his methodology can be found in *No Hiding Place,* by Beth Day (New York: Henry Holt & Co., 1957). His system for active alcoholics involves a stay of eight weeks at Tracy Farms at two hundred dollars a week, though not all clients are required to pay this sum.

In the Beth Day book Tracy is quoted as saying: "It is an entire way of life that we are teaching, not just how to quit drinking. What we try to find is the cause for drinking. When it is realized that drinking comes from the failure to face up to our responsibilities as moral human beings—responsible, ultimately, to our God—then it is easier not to drink than to drink."

The National Council on Alcoholism

A worthwhile source of information on alcoholism is the National Council on Alcoholism, 2 East 103d Street, New York 29, New York. This organization has branches or affiliates in various parts of the United States. By writing to the New York office, you can find out what facilities are nearest to you.

The National Council on Alcoholism (N.C.A.) is separate and distinct from Alcoholics Anonymous, although helpful cooperation exists. In general, N.C.A. conducts activities that are not covered by A.A., such as hospitalization and the like. The financing also is different. A.A. is supported solely by its own members and operates on a minimum budget, while N.C.A. requires considerable sums of money, contributed by the general public and other sources.

Besides N.C.A. there are various state and local organizations dealing with alcoholism. These may be helpful. Check in your telephone book or local directory; or perhaps you can get information from some individual in your community.

The Pill Problem

A number of alcoholics develop addictions or habituations to sedatives, tranquilizers, and perhaps even narcotics, at least at some point in their careers. This creates a bad situation, as the effects of the medicinal agents may become as troublesome and dangerous as the effects of alcohol itself. Drugs misapplied in such a fashion may be *even worse* than alcohol. When both drugs and alcohol are taken at the same time, the results are often extremely bad.

Over the years, A.A. has published a number of pamphlets to cope with this very undesirable situation. The A.A. "party-line" position on "pills" has shifted from time to time, and I shall deal mainly with the most recent A.A. pamphlet *Tranquilizers, Sedatives, and the Alcoholic: Six A.A. Case Histories*, originally printed in 1959 and reprinted in 1961. It is well worth reading.

The point at which I diverge from the viewpoint of this pamphlet is the idea that *all* alcoholics have "addictive personalities" and are therefore in grave danger of addiction to *all* medicinal agents, whether taken on their own volition or prescribed by doctors. In the final analysis, the whole situation is very much an individual one. I am personally addictive to alcohol, but I do not have any tendency to become addicted to anything else.

Intelligent individual judgment is necessary. There are two senseless, irrational extremes to be avoided. One extreme is chronic and constant pill-feeding not based on any real or urgent necessity. Alcoholics and other persons who are perpetually running away from *all* tension, anxiety, and even the mildest discomfort by popping pills down the hatch are probably headed for trouble. It is not absolutely certain, but it is highly probable.

I am sorry to say that this sort of thing is actually promoted by certain medical men and others, who freely hand out all kinds of medication with little regard for the dangers. As a result various addictions and habituations are common—called "iatrogenic" addiction or habituation. This means that the trouble resulted from unwise and ill-advised medical treatment.

The other extreme is represented by the wild-eyed, red-faced, leather-lunged "kill the pill" fanatics who scream like banshees at many, many A.A. meetings, denouncing any and all forms of medication in vociferous tones. The less knowledge these fellows have, the more noise they make. I met one such character who thought that he was very noble, a sort of junior-grade A.A. saint, because he would not take aspirin when he had a headache! Perhaps someone should have awarded him a medal.

In between the two extremes are the mass of A.A. members who from time to time take various forms of medication, even sedatives and tranquilizers, as conditions indicate. Many of them do so with a feeling of uneasiness and at times even shame and guilt because of all the anti-pill tirades they have heard at A.A. meetings. They may think they need the medication, and in some cases they actually do, but often they feel unworthy about taking it. Here again I maintain that the use of any form of medication is very much an individual question. Those who *may* have addictive tendencies toward things other than alcohol had better watch out. Those who do not (as far as they know) have addictive tendencies can probably take almost any form of necessary medication with a clear conscience, but it would be a good plan for them to watch out *too* in order to prevent the possible development of addiction or habituation.

The use of powerful medication to deal with a temporary situation is quite often justified. My own suggestion is to take such medication in the lowest effective doses and for the shortest possible period of time. That approach has worked well for me, and it may work for some others.

Whether the anti-pill fanatics in A.A. like it or not, there are certain chronic diseases that require daily or nearly daily medication over prolonged periods, perhaps for a lifetime. Diabetes could once be controlled only by injections of insulin. Later, drugs were developed (tolbutamide and the like) that will control mild or even moderate diabetes when taken in pill form. If an alcoholic is unlucky enough to have diabetes, he is entitled to take whatever form of antidiabetic pills the doctor prescribes, without interference by A.A. members or anyone else.

There is also epilepsy, which occurs in various forms and which can sometimes be controlled by certain sedatives that prevent epileptic fits. Various potent drugs are used for this purpose. I shall not give a long discourse on epilepsy; but an alcoholic with epilepsy had better discontinue the alcohol and continue whatever antiepileptic medication the doctor tells him to take.

What brought up the epilepsy question is that I once heard (from reliable sources) about an epileptic who was also something of a drunk. When A.A. representatives got in on the act, they got him to stop drinking alcohol but also told him to discontinue his antiepileptic pills. As a result he began throwing fits again. The doctor finally got him to resume the medication for epilepsy; but A.A. earned the reputation with one M.D. of being a low pack of meddling boobs interfering in the field of medical treatment.

And now back to that A.A. pamplet of 1961. My objection to it is that it tends to create an impression that absolutely no one with an alcoholic disturbance can ever safely take sedatives and tranquilizers. Page 24 says: "Just as the alcoholic is unable to use alcohol in a normal, rational mannner, so does he appear unable to limit his consumption of drugs to prescribed limits." That statement is no doubt true of some alcoholics but there is no proof that it is true of all alcoholics. I know several A.A.s in good standing who have taken such agents and have gotten "hooked." They are sad cases. I know others who did not get hooked. When the need for the medication passed, they discontinued it with little or no trouble.

Furthermore, the six A.A. case histories in the pamphlet were all about individuals susceptible to sedatives and tranquilizers. The evidence presented is no doubt true, but it is badly biased and one-sided. I could get hold of six A.A. members not addictive to sedatives and tranquilizers, and then I could cook up a counterblast claiming that pills were wonderful and a splendid way to deal with life's troubles. But I'm not interested in making propaganda either way. I'm trying to get at the facts pro and con, in a level-headed fashion.

If you as an alcoholic are told by a physician to take some sedative or tranquilizer, you had better mention the fact that you are alcoholic and that you do not want to get addicted to anything else. If he still advises you to take the drugs, go ahead, but take them with caution and ask the doctor to please discontinue such medication as soon as he thinks it can be done. That's the most sensible course of action that I can suggest.

Some Ghastly Doggerel to Finish the Book

Back in 1949 when I first made contact with A.A. there was a custom of having four speakers at open meetings. Some of the speakers were very good; but more of them were pretty awful. That was my opinion then and it is my opinion today. The speakers often seemed to be competing to see who could tell the worst horror story. The first speaker might be rather mild, but by the time the meeting got to number four everybody's hair was standing on end. At times, my wife did not sleep all night after I had taken her to hear such such discourses. So she stopped going to the open meetings and never resumed them. I don't blame her.

To ease off my resentment and disgust at the bucket-of-blood boys, I composed some doggerel. When I finally became sober, I showed it around at closed meetings. Some A.A.s thought it was awful. Others thought it was a scream and should get wider circulation. So here it is!

Mike Lowbottom Harangues the Open Meeting

I've sat and listened to low-life tales
From some of you other drunks,
But I'll give you some stuff that will call your bluff—
Compared to ME you were punks!

I started on tea at the age of three,
At five I went on to rum;
I lapped up whisky till I was ten,
When it put me on the bum.

I came home one night from a drunken fight
And me father bawled me out;
I would take no yap from THAT old sap,
So I hit him an awful clout.

Then I got some bricks and a lot of big sticks
And smashed the whole house to bits;
When me mother came home and saw the mess,
She had seven conniption fits.

Over hill and dell, with a yell like hell,
I rushed off into the night;
They could hear me holler for thirteen miles—
It gave the whole town a fright!

Then a drunken sailor I became
And I sailed the seven seas,
Just a rotten bum filled up with rum,
For SOBRIETY didn't please.

With piratical Chinks I would pour down drinks
As we ravaged the China coast;
When I got them drunk, their boats I sunk—
It was always my proudest boast!

And I lived with some bandits in Mexico, too
(Back when I was running guns),
And I still get a fright when I think of the night
When we murdered fourteen nuns!

I used to set fire to cats and dogs
And watch them die in a blaze;
Oh me, oh my, what a hell of a guy
I was in my drinking days!

Yes, a regular devil I became,
I grew two horns and a tail;
I would scare little kids in darkened streets
Just to hear them howl and wail!

Until one day I joined A.A.
And an angel I became!
For something hit me (I don't know what)
And I never was quite the same.

I grew a halo instead of horns,
My tail fell off with a shake;
It flopped around all over the ground,
Then it wiggled away like a snake!

I put on weight, I became sedate,
And I married a beautiful wife;
In SIX WEEKS I was a millionaire
And I thought I was set for life.

But one day strife came into our life
And we argued all one night
On whether we needed that *extra* yacht
And it ended up in a fight.

Oh, she made me mad, and she made me bad
(It was alcoholic thought)—
For I acted wild, just like a child
And I rushed away like a shot!

Then I staggered afar to a soda bar
And I ordered LEMON POP,
For I didn't think, I took that *first drink*
And then I just couldn't stop.

I came to next day, I was miles away
With bugs crawling over my face,
With bloodshot eyes and hideous cries
And with clothes that were a disgrace!

With a yo-heave-ho I took off for Skid Row
Just to follow the life of a bum;
I sold all of my clothes that afternoon
For a half a bottle of rum.

But I didn't care, for I grew some hair
(Just enough to cover me up);
For the Devil looks out for fiends like me,
And I was the Devil's pup!

I drank GASOLINE from the tanks of cars,
I drank TURPENTINE, I drank PAINT;
They are swell when you mix them with kerosene—
You're wrong if you think they ain't.

And I lived in a shack by the railroad track,
Where I hollered all night for fun;
But the cops didn't dare to bother me there,
For I had them all on the run!

If I'd had less guts, I would have gone nuts
And I'd be *insane* today;
But something went *snap* inside my head
And I came back into A.A.

So now I wander from group to group
Giving off horrendous tales;
I tell big lies to other guys—
To women as well as males.

But I'm not so spry, and my end draws nigh,
And I shortly will finish in hell;
Not even A.A. can save me from that,
And perhaps it is just as well.

For the devils will shake, and the devils will quake
And listen in wild amaze
As I scare all hell with the tales I tell
Of me and my drinking days.

The End at Last

I could go on and on with this book until it swelled to the dimensions of an unabridged dictionary; but I don't think that I will. Instead I'll chop it off right here and summarize my contentions in brief.

1. In the present state of knowledge there is no way to deal with a well-advanced alcoholic disturbance except to stop drinking, totally and completely.
2. The current methods of Alcoholics Anonymous have helped thousands of people to stop drinking.
3. On the other hand, there are thousands of other people who have had little or no success with A.A. methods and procedures.
4. In many such cases an approach that is less on the spiritual and moral side and more on the psychological and physiological side can be helpful.
5. It is the purpose of this book to make a start in developing the latter type of approach.
6. Almost anything that succeeds in breaking up a pattern of steady or periodic drinking may be helpful.
7. Thinking about alcoholism and talking about alcoholism is not enough. After talk must come action. You must stop your own drinking; no one else can do it for you. If you do not make some effort yourself, you will never stop drinking.

And with that I leave you.